Voices *from* Louisiana

Voices *from* Louisiana

PROFILES OF CONTEMPORARY WRITERS

Ann Brewster Dobie

Louisiana State University Press
Baton Rouge

Published by Louisiana State University Press

Manufactured in the United States of America
LSU Press Paperback Original
First printing

DESIGNER: *Mandy McDonald Scallan*
TYPEFACE: *Whitman*
PRINTER AND BINDER: *Sheridan Books, Inc.*

Essays on Darrell Bourque, James Lee Burke, Greg Guirard, Julie Kane, William Joyce, and Tom Piazza first appeared in somewhat different form in *Louisiana Cultural Vistas* and are reprinted by permission of the editor.

Library of Congress Cataloging-in-Publication Data

Title: Voices from Louisiana : profiles of contemporary writers / Ann Brewster Dobie.
Description: Baton Rouge : Louisiana State University Press, 2018. | Includes index.
Identifiers: LCCN 2017037225| ISBN 978-0-8071-6891-2 (pbk. : alk. paper) | ISBN 978-0-8071-6892-9 (pdf) | ISBN 978-0-8071-6893-6 (epub)
Subjects: LCSH: American literature—Southern States—History and criticism. | American literature—20th century—History and criticism.
Classification: LCC PS266.L8 V65 2018 | DDC 810.9/9763—dc23
LC record available at https://lccn.loc.gov/2017037225

The paper in this book meets the guidelines for permanence and durability of the Committee on Production Guidelines for Book Longevity of the Council on Library Resources. ♾

Contents

Foreword

A *New York Times* article from April 2015 by Jennifer Moses, "Literary Louisiana," argues that Louisiana "produces writers the way France produces cheese—prodigiously and with world-class excellence." Ann Brewster Dobie's wonderful collection of essays on contemporary Louisiana writers is ample proof of this statement. This generous overview of eleven well-known writers and a handful of newcomers—novelists, short story writers, poets, screenwriters, and nature writers—attests that Louisiana literature is indeed alive and well and flourishing. From the poet-historian and former poet laureate of Louisiana Darrell Bourque to an array of new writers in multiple genres, this volume embodies Louisiana's rich geographical and cultural milieu and speaks to how Louisiana is its own distinct space within the South.

Some of the writers, like Bourque and Ernest Gaines, were born in Louisiana and have made their life's work recovering the voices and stories of the silenced and forgotten; some are associated with a particular region of the state, like New Orleans writer Shirley Ann Grau, whose novels *The House on Coliseum Street* and *The Keepers of the House* explore the complex intersection of race and gender at pivotal times in American and southern history; or James Lee Burke, whose fictional detective Dave Robicheaux shuttles back and forth between New Iberia and New Orleans in the mystery novels that have made Burke's reputation; or Galliano-born Martha Serpas, whose poetry in *The Dirty Side of the Storm* and *Côte Blanche* infuses the Louisiana landscape with a spiritual and mystical light. Some, like Wiley Cash, lived here for a period and were inspired by university classes they took and by Louisiana's strong sense of place; others, like poet Julie Kane and novelist Tom Piazza, are not native to Louisiana but have made their home here and use the state as setting and resource in their works, memorializing Louisiana rituals such as a jazz funeral, or in Piazza's case, writing a post-Katrina novel with sympathy and love for his adopted state.

Dobie is professor emerita of English at the University of Louisiana at Lafayette and editor of three collections of contemporary Louisiana writing—*Something in Common, Uncommonplace,* and—a text I use in my own Louisiana literature class—*Wide Awake in the Pelican State.* She is a writer thoroughly engaged with Louisiana's cultural and literary landscape and attuned to the emerging writers who continue the state's literary narrative. While these essays are aimed at a general audience, they contain enough meat for the seasoned scholar of Louisiana literature and culture, and they taught me some things I didn't know about writers I often read and teach.

One of my favorite essays is "Greg Guirard: A Life on Bayou Amy." Situating this photographer and nature writer in a Thoreauvian context, the essay charts Guirard's quest for a "deliberate" life, his childhood trips with his grandfather in the Atchafalaya Basin, and his deep and abiding environmental concerns as reflected in the books he calls "Cajun documentaries." Both ethnographer and nature writer, Guirard documents in pictures and words a vanishing world of language and landscape, much as Thoreau preached the simple life in the face of a growing American consumer culture.

Considerably more lighthearted than Guirard's elegies for Louisiana's vanishing cultures are Hammond, Louisiana, writer James Wilcox's humorous and satiric renderings of southerners on the edge in his fictional community of Tula Springs, Louisiana. Titles like *Modern Baptists, Polite Sex,* and *Hunk City* suggest a slightly askew world that Wilcox knows well and treats with both humor and compassion. Growing up in Hammond, Wilcox maintains, gave him material enough for a lifetime, some of which came "right out of the newspaper." As the son of a Catholic mother and a Methodist father, Wilcox learned early to straddle that religious divide he works so well in his stories. Reminiscent of southern writers such as Eudora Welty and Rebecca Wells, Wilcox peoples his small town with eccentric characters like Emily Deshotel, "a radiologist who was an authority on stamps and General Custer," and Mrs. Coco, who plays an eighteenth-century cello she bought "in 1959 from a failed waiter in New Orleans who subsequently blossomed out happily as a Mary Kay Cosmetics representative." Beneath the humor of James Wilcox, Ann Dobie argues, is the serious comedy of all great humorists.

This is just a sampling of a rich and varied introduction to contemporary Louisiana writers, a collection that makes us want to return to the original texts and authors. Each essay gives a biographical and literary context for its writer, situating them both in regional and national-international culture. But most of all, each of these essays gives us a taste of the unique gumbo that is Louisiana literature and culture. Kick back and pass a good time with this book. It will educate, entertain, and reward you.

Mary Ann Wilson
James D. Wilson Endowed Professor of Southern Studies
University of Louisiana at Lafayette

Preface

Louisiana is rich in natural resources. It has timber, oil, and natural gas. It grows sugarcane, rice, pine trees, and cotton and has festivals to celebrate them all. Then there are its cultural resources: jazz, Mardi Gras, New Orleans' Garden District, zydeco. An equally valuable resource, though fewer public fêtes are devoted to it, is its writers. All states boast of a few well-known poets or playwrights, or a school of writing that burned brightly for a short time, but Louisiana's poets and fiction makers have long been a part of its history.

Even where literacy was scarce, stories flourished in a strong oral tradition early on, often taking the form of folktales and songs that later would find a home in eighteenth- and nineteenth-century periodicals. Literary conventions emerged in the eighteenth-century poetry of Julien de Lallande Poydras, the nineteenth-century stories of George Washington Cable, Kate Chopin, and Grace King, and the newspaper pieces of Lafcadio Hearn, marking the onset of a notable line of literary artists that includes such luminaries as Arna Bontemps, Moira Crone, Yusef Komunyakaa, Walker Percy, Lyle Saxon, John Kennedy Toole, and more. The list grows longer when those who came for a time and then left, like Sherwood Anderson, William Faulkner, and Robert Penn Warren, are added in.

The making of stories and poems in Louisiana became significant enough to begin publication in the early 1920s of the *Double Dealer,* a New Orleans–based literary journal, and since 1984 the mission has been continued by *Louisiana Literature,* published by Southeastern Louisiana University. The tradition not only continues; it grows as national journals note with favor the fiction, poetry, and creative nonfiction coming from this state.

One of the more remarkable aspects of this tradition is that it has maintained its healthy, some might say robust, character through decades, even centuries. It did not flourish in one period and fade in another. Instead, it has steadily given readers of all genres literary works that please, delight, provoke thought, give insights, and probe the human condition.

The tradition continues with today's Louisiana writers who, like their forebears, try to understand experience by transforming it into story and song. The difference between previous generations and the current one is that the latter is more widely read and, in the case of drama and film, more widely seen. The works of Louisiana's contemporary authors are translated into many languages and distributed throughout the world. They win prestigious prizes. They are studied in classrooms and researched by scholars.

Missing is thoughtful conversation among the general reading public about our state's writers and the literature they produce. By offering insights on eleven well-known authors and an additional essay on some of the newcomers, *Voices from Louisiana* offers the leisure reader, as well as scholars, an opportunity to engage in discussions about them. It is not comprehensive, as there are many highly regarded poets and fiction writers working today who are not included. Indeed, another volume or two would not cover all the established writers or newcomers who are worthy of study. Those who are discussed, however, provide an overview of the contemporary literary landscape. They are poets, filmmakers, novelists, and a nature writer. Some are well-known; some are just beginning their careers. They come from all parts of the state—north and south, city and countryside. In short, they represent a cross section of Louisiana's contemporary literary scene.

The essays are the product of the author's long and abiding interest in Louisiana literature. Its roots in several unique cultures made it attractive initially, but its ability to transcend the local and speak to more universal scenarios, settings, and themes made it increasingly compelling. It became a lifelong study, pushed along by discoveries of new talents that never seemed to end. Such study led to a book-length listing of works by Louisiana writers suitable for classroom use in elementary and secondary school classrooms, magazine articles and scholarly papers, and compilation of three anthologies of works by the state's writers, two of fiction and one of poetry.

In the case of *Voices from Louisiana*, research took a variety of forms. There was the traditional study of written sources that provided a wide range of insights, interpretations, and opinions. Several of the writers graciously consented to personal interviews, sometimes by telephone, sometimes over coffee. Best of all, some of the information and commentaries grew out of personal friendships, relationships that allow one to know more than a biographical profile or conventional interview question can provide.

The reader of this collection of essays is invited to join the author in probing the stories, poems, films, and prose pieces of some of the Louisiana writers who are active today. Together we can examine their literary characteristics, reflect on the ideas they explore, and look at their individual origins to find greater pleasure and a deeper understanding of the world around us.

This book has received support at every step of the way from my writing group: Edward Gauthier, Nettie McDaniel, Lisa Meaux, and Kathleen O'Shaughnessy. I am grateful to them for their many suggestions and constant encouragement. As always, I thank my husband, who brought his keen eye to multiple drafts of the text.

Voices *from* Louisiana

Fallen Beings in an Imperfect World

The Fiction of James Lee Burke

Readers of James Lee Burke's crime novels usually find themselves somewhere between surprise and shock when they meet him for the first time. Unlike the violent men and women whose stories he tells, Burke himself is soft-spoken and polite, given to easy laughter and possessed of a modest demeanor. Different from the best of his characters, who are simply flawed or misguided, and a far cry from the worst, who harbor cruel intentions and commit brutal acts, Burke himself is often described as gentle, quiet, and learned—a sharp contrast to both his hard-bitten, coarse-talking villains who commit the basest of crimes and the equally rough hewn individuals who fight to bring them to justice.

Burke's persona was shaped in part by growing up on the Texas-Louisiana Gulf Coast during the Great Depression, a time of frugality, followed by World War II, a period marked by a scarcity of goods and an abundance of patriotism. For spending money, he and his best friend would go from house to house picking up shoes to shine. Because they only had brown polish, all the shoes were returned brown, but on the positive side, home delivery was free. On the side, he had a supplementary blackberry business.

Education for James Lee Burke came partly from classrooms and partly from life experiences. After high school, he enrolled at Southwestern Louisiana Institute (SLI) as a pre-law student. When his cousin Andre Dubus won first place in a Louisiana college writing contest, Burke decided to enter a story of his own, leading to his first published work, a short story that appeared in the college literary magazine when he was nineteen. After two years at SLI, Burke transferred to the University of Missouri to major in journalism, though he graduated with a bachelor's and a master's degree in creative writing.

Equally important in his education, however, was his postcollege work in a wide variety of fields. After graduation, Burke moved with his wife, Pearl, to Houston, where he continued to write while working on an oilfield pipeline. With the diligence that has come to be a hallmark of his writing process, he managed to complete most of his first novel, *Half of Paradise*, during that period. But that was only the first of Burke's occupations. Later he would work as a newspaper journalist, a land surveyor in Colorado, a rancher, a clerk for the Louisiana Employment Service, an oilfield landman, a reading instructor in the U.S. Job Corps, a member of the U.S. Forest Service in Kentucky, and a social worker with California Parole and Probation on Skid Row in South Los Angeles. He served briefly as writer-in-residence at the University of Southwestern Louisiana (the former SLI, now known as the University of Louisiana at Lafayette) and in 1966 began teaching at the University of Montana. In the 1980s, Burke taught creative writing at Wichita State University. And although he says he isn't particularly knowledgeable about police work, it is worth noting that he taught for nine years at a Miami junior college that served as an extension of the Miami Police Department. Today, after many years living in New Iberia, Louisiana, he and his wife reside in Montana, a landscape that appears frequently in his recent fiction.

The advantage of so many professional and geographical career moves was that they introduced Burke to many sides of America, the admirable and the disreputable, the affluent and the poverty ridden, the sophisticated and the primitive. He worked with criminals, academics, and oilfield hands, and the social inequities he observed were not lost on him. All that experience would sooner or later find its way into his fiction.

Burke has managed to stay remarkably productive throughout his career, partly because of his disciplined, seven-day work week—every week—and partly because he lets a book come to him. Claiming not to understand how creativity works, Burke believes that talent lies outside the self. It is not earned; it is more like a force of nature, something bigger than the individual. Consequently, he accepts stories as if given "by another hand." Similarly, he does not plan out his narratives. They begin with "a feeling of concern, a dilemma of some kind," and then he discovers them as they evolve. Consequently, he says that he cannot claim credit for what he writes (Kowar). Whatever the source, the books keep coming at the rate of about one a year, yielding, in addition to a number of standalone novels, a steady stream of fiction featuring Dave Robicheaux, a second series built around Billy Bob Holland, several narratives based on Hackberry Holland, and two short story collections. Two novels, *In the Electric Mist with Confederate Dead* and *Heaven's Prisoners*, have been made into films.

Despite his prolific production, success has not always seemed inevitable. By the time Burke was thirty-four, he had published three novels, but then he went thirteen years without bringing out a hardback publication. In fact, he shopped *The Lost Get-Back Boogie* for nine years, receiving 110 rejections, apparently an industry record, before Louisiana State University Press put it into print. It was subsequently nominated for the Pulitzer Prize. More critical notice was to follow. In 1988 Burke was given a John Simon Guggenheim Fellowship for Creative Arts in Fiction, and in 2002 he received the Louisiana Writer Award for his contribution to the "literary intellectual heritage of Louisiana." He has been recognized three times by the Mystery Writers of America (MWA): in 1990 the organization presented him with the Edgar Allan Poe Award for Best Novel of the year for *Black Cherry Blues;* in 1998 he received a second "Edgar" for *Cimarron Rose;* and in 2009 the MWA presented him with its Grand Master Award. He has also been the recipient of a Breadloaf Fellowship and a National Endowment for the Arts grant. *In the Moon of Red Ponies* was nominated for both a National Book Award and a Pulitzer Prize.

The success Burke's fiction has had with both critics and readers is undoubtedly due in part to the mystery, suspense, and even the violence that characterize them. Underlying the drama, however, is a deeply thoughtful worldview. Although Burke claims to tell his stories objectively, never manipulating the reader into adopting a particular political or judgmental position, through his realistic settings in a specific time and place, colorful characters with authentic language and attitudes, and powerful descriptions of landscapes, weather, and cities that ring true, one is compelled to see the world as he sees it: how it works, where it errs, and how it should be.

Burke's fictive world is a complex one, full of moral ambiguity, a mixture of brutality and self-sacrifice, malice and love, mortal enemies and loyal friends. The complexity is explored through several recurrent and related topics. Chief among them is the author's distress (approaching anger) over social injustice, whether it takes place on a personal level or on a global scale. Connected to that issue is Burke's sadness at the disappearance of what he sees as a traditional America, including the loss of his own childhood's Cajun culture. Underlying both is the mystery of human corruption and error, along with the promise of redemption that accompanies it. As Burke says: "I believe in redemption. Every great work has dealt with man's quest for redemption, going back to Celtic legend. The linkage between the spirit, the body and divinity is what all human experience is about" (qtd. in Trachtenberg). Not too many years ago, a reader might have been surprised to find such weighty issues and conflicted characters in a piece of crime fiction. In the 1930s and 1940s and even into the 1950s, they would more likely have turned up in what was known as the sociological novel. It is Burke's thinking that fiction that looks at society's antiheroes instead of its heroes, narratives that examine a culture from the bottom up, have assumed the role literary sociology once played. After all, because the wealthiest or most powerful individuals are atypical of a culture, they are not the key to knowing what is going on at any given time. Perhaps recasting the crime novel as a means of understanding a society is one reason Burke's work gets the respect that few other books of the genre receive.

One does not have to read much of Burke's fiction to recognize that it often deals with the challenge of achieving justice in an imperfect world. The wrongdoing usually takes the form of the powerless being exploited or abused by the powerful. It frequently occurs between individuals, but sometimes it takes place between groups of people, the chief case in point being the mistreatment of black Americans by white society, a thematic motif that runs through all his narratives. In *Creole Belle*, it is oil companies that disregard drilling safety to reduce expenses, leading to catastrophic consequences. And *The Tin Roof Blowdown* makes clear that even governments sometimes abuse the people they govern, its first chapter ending with a reference to post-Katrina New Orleans: "That was before one of the most beautiful cities in the Western Hemisphere was killed three times, and not just by the forces of nature." There is no shortage of social inequities in Burke's fictional world or apparently in the one its readers inhabit. All of them are to be fought against.

Related to his antipathy for abuses of power is Burke's longing for a better world, perhaps an ideal one, a world he senses we once had but have lost. In novel after novel, Dave Robicheaux indulges his nostalgia for a world he remembers but no longer experiences. In *The Last Car to Elysian Fields*, in which his friend Clete Purcel accuses him of feeling that "it's always supposed to be 1950," Robicheaux admits: "The world in which I had grown up was gone. I wanted to pretend otherwise, to find excuses for the decay, the strip malls, the trash strewn along the roadways, the century-old live oaks that developers lopped into stumps with almost patriotic pride" (chap. 23). In *The Neon Rain*, he says simply, "I don't like the world the way it is, and I miss the past" (chap. 11). *The Glass Rainbow* and *Creole Belle*, which form one story, deal in part with the rapidly shrinking Louisiana landscape, but the vanishing geography becomes a metaphor for the loss of an era, the death of a traditional America. His attitude is more than mere nostalgia, however. He understands that the complete loss of the past would be devastating because it holds our identity. In *The Neon Rain*, Robicheaux muses, "So we have to resurrect the past constantly, erect monuments to it, and keep it alive in order to remember who we are" (chap. 8).

Robicheaux, a Vietnam veteran, a New Orleans Police Department homicide detective, and later a member of the New Iberia Sheriff's Department, was introduced to readers in 1987 in *The Neon Rain.* Charles Willeford was a crime writer and friend to whom Burke acknowledged a "great debt," saying, "If someone wanted advice about writing, about how to pull it off, how to make it work, punch it up . . . Charles could tell you how to do it" (qtd. in Sublett). In the case of *The Neon Rain,* he recognized the detective's star power after reading only two chapters of the novel, and other readers were quick to follow suit. Robicheaux has by now become so well-known that a festival named for him is held each year in New Iberia, Louisiana, his fictive home. The twentieth book in the series, *Light of the World,* came out in the summer of 2013.

Robicheaux is often described as a flawed hero, his failings evident in the fact that he is a recovering alcoholic, suffers from depression, and struggles with his own violent impulses. Like Burke himself, he lives with anger over the loss of his Cajun culture, fights for the marginalized and ignored members of society, and desires to make the world the way he remembers it to have once been. His battles, then, are twofold: with himself and with the offenders who despoil the natural beauty and goodness of the world.

Burke grows especially expressive when he touches on the destruction of the wetlands of his home state, those marshes and swamps that he remembers as an unspoiled paradise not yet scarred by thousands of miles of canals or polluted by industrial and agricultural rubbish. Speaking of the Atchafalaya Basin of his boyhood, for example, he says: "It was like the Garden of Eden back in those marshes years ago. I thought it was the most beautiful place in the United States. At sunrise there would be this stillness, like the first day of Creation, and the sun looked like cotton candy inside the cypress trees. That's all going down the drain because of what's occurred." Burke was speaking of the devastating British Petroleum oil spill in the spring of 2010. On occasion he grows almost theological in his indictment of society's damage to the ecosystem. "Very few people understand how fragile the wetlands are," he told Mike Di Paolain in 2010. "There's a symbiotic relationship between everything that lives in a marsh, and when you impair it with toxic waste and infuse it with poison, it's like tampering with the work of God." As a reviewer for the *New York Times* once pointed out, "Nobody can touch Burke in the lyrical expression of howling grief" (Stasio).

The concern over social injustice and the longing for a better world have led Burke to consider the nature of evil itself and how humankind is to deal with it. Perhaps, as Robicheaux muses in *The Neon Rain*, southern boys just grow up harboring a dark fascination with man's iniquity. In any case, evil is never far away in Burke's fiction. Some characters make one question if certain people are beyond redemption. In *Creole Belle*, Gretchen Horowitz, Clete Purcel's illegitimate daughter, who works as a professional contract killer, is one such troubling case. The greedy, power-hungry oil companies in that novel are corporate instances of the same indifference to human life and environmental destruction. Sometimes the shadowy nature of characters is underscored by the imagery used to describe them. When Bubba Grimes comes to murder Kippy Jo Pickett in *Heartwood*, he is said to leave "cleft-shaped tracks" in the mud outside her house. But it is the character of Legion Guidry, better known simply as "Legion," a name that carries overtones of biblical demons, who personifies evil most effectively. Appearing in *Jolie Blon's Bounce*, he is callous, repulsive, destructive, and cruel. He is said to speak in an ancient tongue. Having no redeeming characteristics, he carries a mysterious power to unnerve others, leaving one to wonder if people like Legion are irretrievably lost.

In short, Burke's fiction says that we know evil exists, but we cannot explain where it comes from or know how to cope with it, a situation that leaves us fearful and haunted. As Robicheaux comments in *The Tin Roof Blowdown*, "Somewhere out there in the larger world, William Blake's tiger waited to take it all from me" (chap. 27). A natural response to the evil symbolized in Blake's tiger is to take revenge, to fight back. In the same novel Robicheaux explains, "When we feel collectively threatened, or when we are collectively injured, we want the Earp brothers and Doc Holliday on the job and we want the bad guys smoked, dried, fried, and plowed under with bulldozers" (chap. 22). Such a response, however, shows that the tiger is not just "out there" but manifest in our own desire for vengeance. Nobody is exempt from the struggle to rise above ignoble impulses and moral failure.

Although Burke's fiction is remembered by many readers for its graphic (and plentiful) violence, there is redemption too. In his fiction it comes in two forms: one is the human love of family and friends, and the other is traditional Christian belief and practice. The human form is characterized by generosity, loyalty, and forgiveness. It leads one to offer others what one has, "perhaps even bless it with a prayer" (*Black Cherry Blues*, chap. 2), an act that leads to welcome respite from "avarice and deceit and people scamming people and profiting from the desperation and hardship of their fellow Americans" (*Tin Roof Blowdown*, chap. 27). Or, as Robicheaux says at the close of *Creole Belle*, "For me . . . the fact that I can spend my days among the people I love [is] victory enough" (chap. 34).

The theological form of redemption appears in Burke's fiction in both the experiences of its characters and its Christian imagery. In *Black Cherry Blues*, for example, Dave Robicheaux asks a priest to hear his confession. When asked why he seeks absolution, he replies that he doesn't know, then explains: "For my inadequacies. My failures. For any grief or injury I've brought an innocent person. That's the best I can say. I can't describe it" (chap. 8). In the same novel he comments: "As I get older I believe more and more in prayer. At least I feel like I'm dealing with somebody who's got some real authority" (chap. 7). In *Heartwood*, Billy Bob Holland remembers his childhood baptism as a mystical moment in "a private cathedral suffused with stained light that I would always return to in memory when I felt I was unworthy of the world" (chap. 19).

The use of Christian imagery is more mystical. At the end of the short story "Mist" in *Jesus Out to Sea*, for example, Lisa, who has lost her home and her baby in Hurricane Katrina, has a vision in which she sees again her submerged house and then, mysteriously, "tiny lights that remind her of broken Communion wafers inside a pewter chalice or perhaps the souls of infants that have found one another and have been cupped and given safe harbor by an enormous hand." The image brings her "a moment of solace she had not anticipated." A similar instance occurs in a vision Robicheaux has about a wayward young black man toward the end of *The Tin Roof Blowdown:*

> In my fantasy I see Bertrand far out on the water, pulling on the oars, his arms pumped with his task, the ruined City of New Orleans becoming smaller and smaller in the distance, a great darkness spreading across the sky just after sunset. The blisters on his hands turn into wounds that stain the wood of the oars with his blood. As the wind rises and the water becomes even blacker, he sees hundreds if not thousands of lights swimming below the surface. Then he realizes the lights are not lights at all. They have the shape of broken Communion wafers and the luminosity that radiates from them lies in the very fact they have been rejected and broken. But in a way he cannot understand, Bertrand knows that somehow all of them are safe now, including himself, inside a pewter vessel that is as big as the hand of God. (Epilogue)

Burke himself confirms that his work is about the search for redemption. "It's always the story of Golgotha . . . the quest for the Grail," he says. "It's something in the human breast that's always there. That's what I write about" (qtd. in Austin).

Deepening the significance of the spiritual elements of his fiction, and increasing its mysteries too, are the ghosts and dreams and hallucinations that appear in many of Burke's stories, effectively blurring one's sense of reality. Robicheaux explains the interaction of the living and the dead in the epilogue to *The Tin Roof Blowdown*, saying, "I have long subscribed to the belief that the dead lay strong claim on the quick, that indeed their spirits wander and manifest themselves in the middle of our waking day and whisper to us when we least expect it." In the Billy Bob Holland series, the protagonist has long conversations with his late Texas Ranger partner, L. Q. Navarro, and in *In the Electric Mist with Confederate Dead* the reader is never sure whether Robicheaux's conversations with a dead Confederate soldier are real. In *Black Cherry Blues,* Robicheaux talks frequently with his dead wife, Annie, and in *Heartwood* the blind Kippy Jo Pickett "sees pictures in her head" (chap. 3). That is, she sees dead people and has visions of what is going to happen. Burke accounts for the frequent inclusion of mysterious appearances, events, and conversations by pointing out that "the great body of human understanding is in the unconscious, in the world of dreams. That is how we figure out the reality" (qtd. in Rainone).

The characters in Burke's fiction are, not surprisingly, as complex as the situations in which they find themselves. In fact, their inner natures often overshadow the general plot. All of them struggle with demons of one kind or another, and some are not at all what they seem. Burke says there are actually three kinds of wrongdoers in his fiction. The first type of offender is the run-of-the-mill malefactor, losers who get in trouble not because they are violent but because they simply lack the skills to stay within the boundaries of the law. They make bad choices or are corrupted by societal forces such as drugs, the penal system, or poverty (Rainone). Such are most of those who appear in Burke's two short story collections, *The Convict* and *Jesus Out to Sea.* Second are the real sociopaths, vicious creatures who seemingly lack a conscience or human empathy. Legion, the character from *Jolie Blon's Bounce* mentioned earlier, exemplifies this category. The third type consists of those in the mainstream of society who abuse their positions of power, manipulating others for their own profit, without acting illegally. They are people like Earl Deitrich in *Heartwood,* who uses his money and power to control and corrupt much of what happens in Deaf Smith, Texas.

Dave Robicheaux's colorful buddy and colleague Clete Purcel is as politically incorrect as a person can be, and sometimes he seems to have as few moral and ethical scruples as the criminals he opposes. Nevertheless, Purcel does not fall easily into any of the three categories of wrongdoers. He is a loyal friend who saves Robicheaux time after time. Burke describes the pair as descendants of Don Quixote and Sancho Panza in the ways in which they complement each other. "The two of them," he says, "form a third personality that's quite formidable" (qtd. in Rainone). Robicheaux sums up their relationship: "Clete protected the innocent and tried to do good deeds for people who had no voice, and I tried to care for my family and not brood upon the evil that men do. We didn't change the world, but neither were we changed by it" (*Creole Belle*, epilogue).

A second, less celebrated cast of characters was introduced ten years later with the novel *Cimarron Rose*, featuring Billy Bob Holland, a Texas Ranger who becomes a lawyer in Deaf Smith, Texas, and later in Missoula, Montana. There are distinct similarities between Billy Bob and Dave Robicheaux. Both champion the downtrodden, agonize over personal weaknesses and errors, and struggle with violent tendencies. Both want the world to be a better place. Only the landscape changes.

Playing a role that is every bit as significant as those the characters enact, nature in all its power and beauty extends the reader's understanding of humankind's capacity for cruelty and malice, society's inequities, and a corrupted world. In contrast to the ugliness and pain created by both the mean-spirited and the merely imperfect beings who make up our world, nature, left alone, remains unblemished. Enhanced by the lyricism of Burke's descriptions, it reminds the reader that all is not lost. Consider, for example, his lush depiction of Bayou Lafourche in *The Neon Rain:* "The shore was thickly lined with cypress trees, and it was cool and quiet in the green-gold morning light that fell through the canopy of limbs overhead. The lily pads were abloom with purple flowers, and I could smell the trees, the moss, the wet green lichen on the bark, the spray of crimson and yellow four-o'clocks that were still open in the shade" (chap. 1). Fallen beings though we are, redemption remains possible. As the quotation from Ecclesiastes that closes *Creole Belle* says, "One generation passeth away, and another generation cometh: but the earth abideth forever."

Regardless of where the narrative is set, Burke draws the reader into the locale through his descriptions of the natural world. Consider, for example, what he does with Montana in *Bitterroot:* "[I] drove out on the Clark Fork west of town in a sun shower and sat on an enormous flat rock that slanted into the water. The river was wide, the color of green-tarnished copper, and cottonwoods dotted the banks and there were blue mountains in the distance" (chap. 16). Even urban scenes remind the reader of the goodness to be had. In "Jesus Out to Sea," for example, the narrator recalls the New Orleans of his boyhood: "You woke in the morning to the smell of gardenias, the electric smell of the streetcars, chicory coffee, and stone that has turned green with lichen. The light was always filtered through trees, so it was never harsh, and flowers bloomed year-round. New Orleans was a poem, man, a song in your heart that never died."

Adding to the significance of the themes are Burke's frequent allusions to literature, history, and philosophy. As he is widely read and well educated, it is not unusual to find references to Bruegel, Ernest Hemingway, John Milton, William Shakespeare, Voltaire, and more—not the usual citations made in crime fiction. Claiming that he was influenced by Chaucer, Don Quixote, and the Arthurian legends, he says, "I think the greatest single aid to a writer is some appreciation of classical literature, [such as] the Renaissance and mythology" (qtd. in Rainone). Obviously, he follows his own recommendation that one should "never read bad stuff if you're an artist; it will impair your own game" ("James Lee Burke's Quotes"). His own reading is evident in the wide vocabulary he uses. It is not unusual to find words such as *succubus* or *libidinous personality* scattered through his narratives.

When asked what is important for aspiring writers to know, James Lee Burke describes his own lifelong practice. He says: "An artist must ignore the naysayers and not be discouraged by rejection and never, under any circumstances, give up submitting one's work. My rule has always been that no manuscript stays at home more than 36 hours. If a person has to ask the opinion of others about his work, in all probability the work is no good. An artist creates out of compulsion and will continue to do so until his death" (Burke website).

PUBLISHED WORKS BY JAMES LEE BURKE

DAVE ROBICHEAUX SERIES

The Neon Rain (1987)
Heaven's Prisoners (1988)
Black Cherry Blues (1989)
A Morning for Flamingos (1990)
A Stained White Radiance (1992)
In the Electric Mist with Confederate Dead (1993)
Dixie City Jam (1994)
Burning Angel (1995)
Cadillac Jukebox (1996)
Sunset Limited: A Novel (1998)
Purple Cane Road: A Novel (2000)
Joli Blon's Bounce: A Novel (2002)
Last Car to Elysian Fields: A Novel (2003)
Crusader's Cross (2005)
Pegasus Descending (2006)
The Tin Roof Blowdown (2007)
Swan Peak (2008)
The Glass Rainbow (2010)
Creole Belle (2012)
Light of the World (2013)

BILLY BOB HOLLAND SERIES

Cimarron Rose: A Novel (1997)
Heartwood: A Novel (1999)
Bitterroot (2001)
In the Moon of Red Ponies: A Novel (2004)

HACKBERRY HOLLAND SERIES

Lay Down My Sword and Shield (1971)
Rain Gods (2009)
Feast Day of Fools: A Novel (2011)
House of the Rising Sun: A Novel (2015)
The Jealous Kind: A Novel (2016)

WELDON HOLLAND SERIES

Wayfaring Stranger: A Novel (2014)

SHORT STORY COLLECTIONS

The Convict: Stories (1985)
Jesus Out to Sea: Stories (2007)

MISCELLANEOUS

Half of Paradise: A Novel (1965)
To the Bright and Shining Sun (1970)
The Lost Get-Back Boogie: A Novel (1978)
Two for Texas (1982)
White Doves at Morning: A Novel (2002)
The Jealous Kind: A Novel (2016)

WORKS CITED

Austin, Keith. "The Big Uneasy." *Sydney Morning Herald*, March 15, 2008, *www.smh.com.au/news/books/the-big-uneasy/2008/03/14/html.*

Burke, James Lee. Author's website, jamesleeburke.com.

———. *Bitterroot.* New York: Simon & Schuster, 2001. Kindle edition.

———. *Black Cherry Blues.* New York: Little, Brown, 1989. Kindle edition.

———. *Creole Belle.* New York: Simon & Schuster, 2012. Kindle edition.

———. *Heartwood.* New York: Dell Publishing, 1999. Kindle edition.

———. "Jesus Out to Sea." *Jesus Out to Sea: Stories.* New York: Simon & Schuster, 2007. Kindle edition.

———. *The Last Car to Elysian Fields: A Novel.* New York: Simon & Schuster, 2003. Kindle edition,

———. "Mist." *Jesus Out to Sea: Stories.* New York: Simon & Schuster, 2007. Kindle edition.

———. *The Neon Rain.* New York: Simon & Schuster, 1987. Kindle edition.

———. *The Tin Roof Blowdown.* New York: Simon & Schuster, 2007. Kindle edition.

Di Paolain, Mike. "Wetlands a Garden of Eden before Spill, Says Novelist." *Irish Times,* June 22, 2010, www.irishtimes.com/news/wetlands-a-garden-of-eden-before-spill-says-novelist-1.681438.

"James Lee Burke's Quotes." QuoteHD.com, www.quotehd.com/quotes/author/james-lee-burke-author-quotes-and-sayings.

Kowar, Kacey. "Interview with James Lee Burke." Kacey Kowars Show, December 8, 2015, http://jamesleeburke.com/kacey-kowers-interview-with-jlb/.

Rainone, Anthony. "Jammin' with James Lee Burke." *January Magazine,* October 2004, http://januarymagazine.com/profiles/jlburke.html.

Stasio, Marilyn. "James Lee Burke's 'Creole Belle,' and More." *New York Times,* July 20, 2012, www.nytimes.com/2012/07/22/books/review/james-lee-burkes-creole-belle-and-more.html.

Sublett, Jesse. "One of the Great Ones." *Austin Chronicle,* November 6, 1998, www.austinchronicle.com/books/1998-11-06/520551/.

Trachtenberg, Jeffrey A. "The Craze after the Storm: James Lee Burke's Dark Look at Post-Katrina New Orleans." *Wall Street Journal,* August 17, 2007, https://www.wsj.com/articles/SB118729506160800041.

The Fictive World of Ernest Gaines

In a personal reminiscence, Ernest Gaines recalls that when he moved to Vallejo, California, at the age of fifteen, his uncle gave him a choice of spending his summer by taking up boxing or by reading. It did not take long for him to leave the ring for the library, where, to his youthful surprise, he found that it was full of books about the lives of white people and woefully short on books about the lives of African Americans. Until then he had not realized that few books by black writers were available because, growing up as a black child on the River Lake Plantation in Oscar, Louisiana, where his parents were workers, he could not check out books from the library. (Gaines would join his parents in the fields when he was eight years old.) Even when he enrolled in Vallejo Junior College in the early 1950s, few narratives based on the experiences of African Americans had joined the mainstream. He remembers that when he attended San Francisco State College and later Stanford, on a Wallace Stegner Fellowship to study creative writing, he was asked to read only passages from *Native Son*, and Ralph Ellison's *Invisible Man* was newly published and just becoming known. Since that time, Gaines's life has been spent filling the literary void.

Gaines's depictions of black families and experiences in eight novels and countless short stories represented for the reading public a glimpse into what was virtually a new world for them, one that literature had largely overlooked. When *The Autobiography of Miss Jane Pittman* and *A Gathering of Old Men* were made into televised movies, public awareness of the pressures, practices, and traditions of that world was further expanded and deepened. They introduced the audience to a culture many had not met in fiction before.

The paucity of fiction by African Americans meant that Gaines had few models to guide him during his development as a writer; black writers had little influence on him as he learned his craft. Instead, he had to draw his narratives and their characters from personal experience, family stories, African American culture, southern tradition, and his own imagination. Having listened as a child to the stories of the old people, Gaines understands his culture's assumptions about family, attitudes, behavior, and values. From his early childhood experiences, he developed a sense of what it means to love the land but not own it, to live in former slave quarters in the shadow of the plantation house, to attend school and church in the same building, and to have to move to another town to continue his education. He was able to re-create that world in his fiction because he carried in his memory such a strong sense of place—the land, its people, and its culture. Consequently, most of his work is set in rural Louisiana among the poor, black, bilingual populace of his native Pointe Coupee Parish. In describing his identity in an interview with Marcia Gaudet and Carl Wooton, Gaines said:

> I see myself as a writer, and I happen to have been born here [Louisiana]. I was born black. I was born on a plantation. I've lived in that interracial, or ethnic, mixture of the Cajun, and the big house owned by the Creoles—not Cajuns, but Creoles—and the blacks. I was associated very early with the Baptist church; I was christened as a Baptist. But I went to Catholic school, a little school in New Roads, my last three years in Louisiana. I had to go through their kind of discipline. I had to go to mass. I didn't go to confession or anything like that. I didn't take the Holy Sacrament. I had to go through all these kinds of things. My aunt who raised me and who was crippled spoke Creole. Some of the old ladies on the plantation and some of the old men spoke Creole. (80)

Gaines's deep sense of place was expanded when his young adulthood presented him with a broader context, one that included other races and ethnic groups and different relations between social classes. Moving to California as a young man introduced him to books and cities and a new world of experiences that would allow him to understand more clearly the nature of his own culture and the circumstances that had forged it. His respect for the strength of the people of the quarter, combined with his knowledge of that bigger world in which the social dictates and rules of decorum were different, allowed Gaines to depict the limitations imposed on his characters without dishonoring their dignity. As a result, his fiction illuminates the experience of people who up until its appearance had been mostly ignored, certainly underrepresented, and sometimes misrepresented in literature.

The uniqueness of varied cultures is developed by Gaines through their many voices. Most audible in his fiction are the voices of rural African Americans. On the level of authenticity of expression, they resonate with rhythms and idioms that differ from those of urban America and white America. Gaines acknowledges that he absorbed these patterns as a child, listening to the stories people told while sitting on the porch or gathered around the fireplace at night. He said, "I came from a place where people sat around and chewed sugarcane and roasted sweet potatoes and peanuts in the ashes and sat on ditch banks and told tales and sat on porches and went into the swamps and went into the fields—that's what I came from" (qtd. in Gaudet and Wooton 37). That was not urban. Those situations were not the ones James Baldwin was writing about. They were voices not heard before in American literature.

Gaines's ability to catch the sound of these people talking was enhanced by his technical training and literary background. As Gaudet and Wooton point out: "Though he bases his narrative on the folk storytelling tradition, he is quite obviously not a folk storyteller. He is an artist who recognizes the value of the language and customs of his culture, and who consciously manipulates that material through techniques and in forms that occupy the mainstream of western literary tradition" (5). Consequently, Gaines is able to give readers not just black discourse but varieties of black discourse, not a one-dimensional perspective but conflicting and overlapping ones that deepen the authenticity of the portrayal. *A Gathering of Old Men*, for example, uses multiple narrators who represent different segments of its plantation world. Each tells the story in his or her unique way. Even his frequently anthologized story "The Sky Is Gray" has characters who represent differing speech patterns within the black community. Most obvious among them are the preacher and a revolutionary young man who meet in a dentist's waiting room. The young narrator, James, recounts the incident using his own manner of speech:

> This one here's sitting on the same side me and Mama's sitting, and he is kind of sitting in front of that preacher. He looks like a teacher or somebody that goes to college. He's got on a suit, and he's got a book that he's been reading. "We don't question is exactly our problem," he says. "We should question and question and question—question everything."
>
> The preacher just looks at him a long time. He done put a toothpick or something in his mouth, and he just keeps on turning it and turning it. You can see he don't like that boy with that book.
>
> "Maybe you can explain what you mean," he says.
>
> "I said what I meant," the boy says. "Question everything. Every stripe, every star, every word spoken. Everything."
>
> "It 'pears to me that this young lady and I was talking about God, young man," the preacher says.
>
> "Question Him, too," the boy says.
>
> "Wait," the preacher says. "Wait now."
>
> "You heard me right," the boy says. "His existence as well as everything else. Everything."
>
> The preacher just looks across the room at the boy. You can see he's getting madder and madder. But mad or not mad, the

> boy ain't thinking 'bout him. He looks at that preacher just's hard's the preacher looks at him.
>
> "Is this what we educating them for?" the preacher says. "Is this what we educating them for?"
>
> "You're not educating me," the boy says. "I wash dishes at night so that I can go to school in the day. So even the words you spoke need questioning."
>
> The preacher just looks at him and shakes his head.
>
> "When I come in this room and seen you there with your books, I said to myself, 'There's an intelligent man.' How wrong a person can be." (Sec. 7)

Not only do the preacher and the young man represent contrasting views, finally coming to blows over their differences, but they also reflect the diversity that results from education. Whereas some of Gaines's characters are probably illiterate, others study and question. They face the world with different expectations and different defenses, though all of them are closely bound together in rural black culture, which, Gaines shows, is not a single body of stereotypical characteristics.

In addition to introducing the discourse of rural, poor, southern, black America, Gaines provides depictions of another lesser-known culture, one composed of people of Creole and Cajun lineage. Kate Chopin, who drew characters and settings from the communities of French and Spanish descendants in Louisiana, had been largely forgotten by the time Gaines began writing. Although her stories, and certainly her novel *The Awakening*, would later find popularity with readers, in the early 1960s the Cajun and Creole cultures were little known to most people who lived outside them. The manner of speech of their members had been seldom heard or noticed.

Discourses other than those reflecting the black, Creole, and Cajun cultures are also evident in Gaines's fiction. He acknowledges a number of significant influences on his writing that came from beyond the black community, in particular the radio shows of the

1950s, "where you can only hear things and they tell you what's going on." There was also the jazz saxophonist Lester Young, who, Gaines points out, instead of playing on the note, "plays around the note, or under the note, or above the note" (personal interview). Voices from other cultures were important too. White writers (William Faulkner, F. Scott Fitzgerald, Ernest Hemingway, Ivan Turgenev, Mark Twain) and the jumbled California culture (made up of blacks, Latinos, Filipinos, Japanese, Chinese, and whites) all played a part in the world Gaines writes about and from. His fiction presents no single language but rather a welter of complementary and conflicting and overlapping ones, just as one finds in society.

Although Gaines is not generally thought of as a "political writer," his world, and by extension his work, could not escape being influenced by the turbulence of the times in which he lived. When he was in his early twenties, the denial of African Americans' rights to schools and universities (education), the voting booth (political power), and lunch counters (social intercourse) was under siege. In 1957 federal troops were sent to Little Rock, Arkansas, to ensure desegregation of its high school. Lyndon B. Johnson's War on Poverty began in 1964, and his Great Society, enacted by legislation introduced in 1965, established programs such as Medicare and Medicaid. Thurgood Marshall, who over a decade earlier had won the *Brown v. Board of Education* case that led to the integration of public schools, became the first black justice appointed to the U.S. Supreme Court in 1967. The Civil Rights Act of 1968, stressing open housing, was on the horizon. Newspapers, magazines, and television news routinely reported changes in the social system that had been in place since the Civil War. In short, African Americans' limited access to opportunity and an inequitable division of power were being questioned at the same time Gaines's stories and novels appeared in bookstores across the country. The issues would inevitably make their way into his fiction.

In "The Sky Is Gray," for example, the young black boy James and his family lack the rights taken for granted by white members of society. They are powerless. They do not even live close to centers of power where they might catch the notice of those who could change the dynamics of their situation. In fact, at the time of the story, legal and social measures were firmly secured to keep blacks "in their place." Through the practice of segregation, maintained by those who have power, James and his family will remain powerless because of poverty, ignorance, and separation from the mainstream. He and his mother sit in the bus behind the sign that says "Colored." When the dentist goes to lunch, they must leave his waiting room, and to find food and shelter from the cold, they go "back of town," passing by whites-only cafés but not looking in. By law and by social practice, the two of them have no choice but to endure. In such a context the story becomes a quietly compelling document, testifying to social wrongs that cry out for attention and change.

Gaines's fiction could never be described as overtly supporting or undermining particular ideologies. His narratives have not been conceived as explicitly political documents. Nevertheless, his poignant depictions of southern, rural, black society challenge the power structure of the segregated society they depict. His stories and novels recognize the complexity of human interaction, both intraracial and interracial, while holding up models of what is possible, even in a society built on wildly unequal divisions of power. And although many of the legal strictures and mores of the narrative settings have radically changed in the decades since his works' publication, they still manage to touch the emotions and the sense of ethics of contemporary readers, reminding them of what was and what must never be again.

Several specific themes grow out of the tension between the world as Gaines knew it as a child, his sense of place, and social changes impacting it. The most evident one, perhaps, is the search for manhood, a manhood characterized by dignity that cannot be impugned by circumstances. In *A Lesson before Dying*, a novel set in a small Cajun community, the local African American teacher visits Jefferson, a young man convicted of a murder in which he had no intended role. He goes at the request of two of the older women in the community to share his learning with the imprisoned man and to give him a sense of pride as he awaits his execution. Both men grow in stature as together they find respect in resisting dehumanizing social forces. They learn to survive with dignity in a harsh world that systematically tries to deny them their manhood. Speaking to the teacher after the execution has taken place, a witness to it comments on Jefferson's composure at the end, saying: "He was the strongest man in that crowded room, Grant Wiggins. . . . He was, he was. I'm not saying this to make you feel good. I'm not saying this to ease your pain. Ask that preacher, ask Harry Williams. He was the strongest man there. We all stood jammed together, no more than six, eight feet away from that chair. We all had each other to lean on. When Vincent asked him if he had any last words, he looked at the preacher and said, 'Tell Nannan I walked.' And straight he walked, Grant Wiggins. Straight he walked. I'm a witness. Straight he walked" (253–54).

Another of Gaines's themes deals with tensions between those who are no longer willing to accept the societal limitations they have inherited and others who defend the power structure that has been in place since the Civil War. In *A Gathering of Old Men*, for example, Gaines depicts both those who are committed to the status quo and those who embrace change. On the one hand are Jack Marshall, part owner of the Marshall plantation, and his wife, Bea, who embody the old plantation order. Jack is drunk throughout the entire novel, and Bea is the useless mistress of their declining plantation. Another aspect of outdated attitudes is evident in Fix Bouton, a violent man whose treatment of blacks is harsh and unrestrained. Although his day is past, he continues to hold on to his outdated attitudes and beliefs. On the other hand, there is his son Gil, a star football player at Louisiana State University, who depends on his black teammate Cal for success on the playing field. So bonded are they that the public refers to them as "Salt and Pepper." Gil's attitudes do not change when the game is done. He argues forcefully for the rule of law in response to the murder that propels the story, thereby putting forth a vision of a new social order that has harmonious and interdependent race relations. The verdict that is handed down in the ensuing legal proceedings suggests that Gil's voice will ultimately prevail. The defendants, both black and white, are placed on five years' probation, pointing out that the legal status of the races has been altered in the South.

The image of the rising black generation is Snookum, a male child whose youth and vitality stand in contrast to the old men. But even they have broken with the past by assembling with guns for their mutual defense. The most significant assertion of redefined black masculinity, however, comes from Charlie, the murderer, who initially acts out of cowardice and runs away from the shooting but later courageously returns to confess to the crime and die in a gunfight with Luke, the leader of a potential lynching party. Charlie grows into his manhood.

Finally, there is the question of identity. How does the black individual define himself or herself? In another short story from *Bloodline*, "A Long Day in November," the character Munford says that white people need people like himself, people of color, to prove they are human. They see black people and know what they are not. In a culture that has traditionally required that a person belong to one race or another, is the black man to do the same? The answer seems to lie in recognizing that although one honors his cultural background, one's identity transcends racial designation. It requires acting responsibly and with integrity, traits not given to one race or another. Gaines explains the situation when speaking of himself:

> I know who I am. I know that I was born in Pointe Coupee Parish. I know that I grew up on a plantation. I know about the old people around me who sacrificed everything for me to educate me. I know that I have written books. I know that my books have been translated into many languages. I know all these things about myself. I know that I care for my family. I know that I care for my friends. I know that I don't give a

> damn for my enemies. I know that I don't judge all whites as my enemies; I don't judge them as my friends, either. I know I have white friends. I don't say that all blacks are my friends, because I don't have too many black friends here . . . . I say I must go on and do my work, I must earn my living, I must do my teaching yet communicate with my friends, be with my friends, and all this sort of thing. (Gaudet and Wooton 54)

Although Gaines does not talk about his work in political terms and generally asserts that he does not write for any particular audience, he has on occasion admitted that he would like to think that he writes for the black youth and the white youth of the South. Never interested in publishing just for money, just to sell books, he has stated that his purpose is to produce good writing, and if that touches young people who will make a better world than their predecessors experienced, he will be pleased.

Despite disclaimers about making money, however, economics has influenced publication of Gaines's fiction. His first novel, *Catherine Carmier*, went little noticed, making the stories he subsequently submitted unattractive to publishers. To get them into print, he had to produce a second novel. Even then there seemed to be little recognition—except on the part of Dorothea Oppenheimer, who became Gaines's agent and close friend—of his artistry, authenticity, and power. Today it is difficult to realize that perceptive editors did not recognize the relationship his work would go on to have with audiences over time. Now frequently anthologized and taught in schools and colleges, Gaines's works have not only opened up African American culture for all the world to see. They have also given readers the optimism to believe in social change. His fictive world exists as a historical document of what once was, continues to offer political challenge to unbalanced power structures, and poses a model of interracial accord.

The works of Ernest Gaines have more than filled the literary void he knew as a young man.

PUBLISHED WORKS BY ERNEST J. GAINES

BOOKS

Catherine Carmier (1964)
Of Love and Dust (1967)
Bloodline (1968)
The Autobiography of Miss Jane Pittman (1971)
In My Father's House (1978)
A Gathering of Old Men (1983)
A Lesson before Dying (1993)
Mozart and Leadbelly: Stories and Essays (2005)

SHORT STORIES

"The Turtles" (1956)
"Boy in the Double Breasted Suit" (1957)
"Mary Louis" (1960)
"Just like a Tree" (1963)
"The Sky Is Gray" (1963)
"A Long Day in November" (1964)
"My Grandpa and the Haint" (1966)

FILMOGRAPHY

The Autobiography of Miss Jane Pittman (1974)
The Sky Is Gray (1980)
A Gathering of Old Men (1987)
A Lesson before Dying (1999)

WORKS CITED

Chopin, Kate. *The Awakening.* New York: Simon & Schuster, 1996.

Gaines, Ernest. *A Gathering of Old Men.* New York: Knopf, 1983.

———. *A Lesson before Dying.* New York: Vintage Books, 1993.

———. "The Sky Is Gray." *Bloodline.* New York: Vintage Books, 1968. Kindle edition.

Gaudet, Marcia, and Carl Wooton. *Porch Talk with Ernest Gaines: Conversations on the Writer's Craft.* Baton Rouge: Louisiana State University Press, 1990.

Darrell Bourque

Poet and Poetry Advocate

Louisiana's long tradition of story and song is no less vibrant today than it was in the past. Much of its vitality comes from writers themselves who lend their energies to the promotion of its literature. They give workshops, speak in schools, give readings, and serve on discussion panels. On one day each fall, the Louisiana Book Festival, sponsored by the Louisiana Center for the Book in the State Library of Louisiana, brings authors together with their counterparts, their readers, to celebrate their mutual love of books and reading.

One of those in the vanguard of showcasing Louisiana's literature is Darrell Bourque, one of the state's former poet laureates. Since his appointment to the post by Governor Kathleen Blanco in 2007 and reappointment in 2009 by Governor Bobby Jindal, Bourque has made countless presentations in an effort to see that our state's stories and poems, especially its poems, receive the attention of both writers and readers. "Being poet laureate," he says, "gives you opportunities to have conversations with people who would not ordinarily be talking about poetry" (personal interview, 2012).

Over the past several years, Bourque has given workshops for fourth graders in New Iberia, met with graduate students from Chatham University of Pittsburgh who were visiting Louisiana on a Writing Field Seminar, read from his own work at Poets House in New York City, and delivered the address at the first meeting of the National English Honor Society at Lafayette High School. During the school year, he conducts weekend retreats for Louisiana Writing Project teachers and works throughout the year with the NUNU Arts and Culture Collective. He regularly sits on panels at the Louisiana Book Festival in Baton Rouge to discuss the state's literature and its writers and for several years read poems on a weekly program produced by the National Public Radio station in Lafayette. Even when Governor Jindal neglected to reappoint Bourque to finish out his term in the early months of 2008, he continued his readings and presentations. Gone is the crown of laurel leaves that the ancient Greek tradition dictated a laureate should wear to signify his eminence, but the mission remains much the same as it has been over the centuries: Darrell Bourque works to promote the reading and writing of poetry.

His mission has a long and venerable history created by his Louisiana predecessors, such as Pinkie Gordon Lane and Brenda Marie Osbey, and has been continued by those who have succeeded him in the post, such as Julie Kane and Ava Leavell Haymon. They are all in good company with other poets laureate who are neither local nor contemporary, such as Petrarch, who in 1341 accepted the invitation of Rome over the one he received from Florence. Ben Jonson unofficially served the court of King James I in the seventeenth century, and John Dryden, in 1668, was the first to accept the formal title in England. The duties of the position varied with time and place, sometimes requiring the poet to commemorate royal birthdays and marriages or to celebrate a public event such as a military victory, but at other times calling for him to do little more than give readings of his works. The rewards varied, too. In the English system, monetary compensation was usually supplemented by a fixed annual portion of wine.

It was not until 1937, however, that the United States moved to create the post by appointing a consultant in poetry. Almost fifty years later, the title was changed to poet laureate consultant in poetry to the Library of Congress. The names of the writers who have been so honored are familiar even to readers who are not poetry fans—names such as Elizabeth Bishop, Billy Collins, Robert Frost, and Robert Penn Warren. Along the way various states, including this one, created their own laureates. In Louisiana the selection process is governed by a statute that requires the Louisiana Endowment for the Humanities (LEH) to appoint a committee composed of two published poets who live in the state, two professors of literature from a state college or university, two representatives from LEH, and a representative from Louisiana State University Press. After deliberation, the committee submits three names to the governor, who chooses one to serve for a term of two years. The poet laureate's sole required duty is to present one public reading a year. There is no wine allotment in return.

Active poets laureate can link artists, educational institutions, and the general public—constituencies that often remain isolated from each other. In a school, for example, practicing poets can show that poetry is connected to students' lives in powerful, significant ways, share the excitement that comes from dealing with language, and demonstrate its vitality. In other venues they can bring the same message to the general public, reminding people of how poetry celebrates the grand events of our lives and how it consoles us at times of sadness and loss. In short, the work of today's poet laureate is to bring the good news to people of all ages that poetry is not some classroom mystery that one must get through from time to time but a natural human activity that allows one to live fully.

Bourque's early years did not suggest that he would become a poet. Growing up in Church Point, Louisiana, he lived in a family neighborhood surrounded by aunts, grandparents, cousins, and siblings, nearly all of whom spoke French as well as English. The adults turned to French for conversations with each other, including exchanges with neighbors, but spoke English to the children. Only Bourque's great-grandmother, with whom he lived for a time during his high school years, refused to speak English and used French when addressing the children.

The family lived on his grandfather's property, a special enclave where everybody not only knew each other but lived with each other from time to time. When he was a child, there were plenty of other children to play with, and later there were house dances where everyone gathered for fun. He recalls, "All the people I grew up with were doing all they could to give me what I needed to move into a life that would be satisfying to me" (personal interview, 2016). What was missing was easy access to books and education and art.

With high school graduation it became clear that Bourque was expected to orchestrate his own life. There were no expectations that he would have to fulfill, and there would be no help for him to go to college. He was on his own to figure out what the rest of his life would hold. Looking back, he sees the limited academic resources of his childhood to have been fortuitous because his hunger for literature, music, and travel forced him to reach beyond the comfortable environment of home and family to find them. He credits the rich cultural environment of his early years with giving him the courage to pursue what he wanted. "Everything that could be seen as a limitation," he says, "was matched by a community and familial environment characterized mainly by openness and lack of impediment" (personal interview, 2015).

In time, the experiences he dreamed of would be his, but the route would not be without its detours. While puzzling out how to leap from his rural South Louisiana childhood to a world he could at that point only imagine, he took various jobs—all of them unrelated to poetry. The first year after high school, he worked as a deliveryman for Clover Farm Creamery. Rising before dawn every morning, he dutifully deposited white bottles on doorsteps throughout Lafayette. That was the upside. The downside was that never having driven a truck before, within two months he had managed to knock so many of the glass bottles out of their crates that he had to quit the job and take out a loan to pay for their breakage. To pay off the loan, he became a shoe salesman in Opelousas. Things were getting worse instead of better. Realizing that something had to change, in 1961 he rented a room in Sunset, Louisiana, and began to commute to the University of Southwestern Louisiana.

His years as a college student did not lead any more directly to poetry than his milk deliveries had. Because he was highly visual, his first notion was to study architecture, but by the second semester at the university, his love of reading had pulled him to the liberal arts and eventually to English. With the change of major, Bourque found himself caught up in the English Department's intense interest in drama. When he did get around to writing a poem, it was not by choice. It was in response to a classroom assignment to compose a lyric poem modeled on those of Wordsworth. He continued his work in drama through his master's degree, even writing for his thesis a comic adaptation of Dryden's tragicomedy *The Spanish Friar*, a play he eventually produced for the Lafayette Little Theater.

He might have stayed with the genre had it not been that Florida State University (FSU), where he went to work on his PhD, had few courses dealing with dramatic literature. It did have courses in creative writing though, and Bourque enrolled in them and began to write poems, although he intended to focus on literary criticism. When he ran into problems with his dissertation director, a not unusual occurrence for a doctoral student, he returned to Lafayette with a five-year deadline for completing the degree. In the fifth year, just as the time limit was approaching, Florida State instituted a creative writing degree, and he submitted a volume of poems, composed of pieces begun in classes at FSU along with others he had written in his five years away from campus, as his dissertation. Van Brock, his new director, subsequently brought out an anthology that included Bourque's first published poem.

With the degree in hand, Bourque returned to the University of Louisiana at Lafayette, where he eventually became professor of English and served as department head, coordinator of interdisciplinary humanities, director of creative writing, and even director of freshman English. And he continued writing poems, eventually publishing multiple volumes of poetry, some of the most recent of which are a chapbook entitled *Holding the Notes*, *Megan's Guitar and Other Poems*, and *Where I Waited*. He has participated in several collaborative projects, such as *Call and Response: Conversations in Verse*, written with poet Jack Bedell. His current project is to reawaken public notice of the almost forgotten musician Amédé Ardoin, whose recordings of Cajun and Creole songs significantly influenced performers who followed. Ardoin died in 1942 in a racial assault in central Louisiana and was buried in an unmarked grave. In a personal interview with Bourque, he admits that today, with all these poems behind him, he still marvels at the birth of new ones, coming as they do like small miracles of creation.

Bourque's poems come from several different sources. Many of them begin to form while he is on his morning run in the countryside near his home in Church Point, where he still lives. As a lifelong practice, running has meditative as well as physical dimensions for him. Like Wallace Stevens, who composed his poems as he walked to and from his work at an insurance office, Bourque waits for the physical exercise to suggest the poem. And since he runs on the same property where he played as a child, crossing from one boundary of his grandfather's land to another, past the houses and borders he has known so long, memory comes to life. The mind is put at ease. A poem begins to form.

About half of his poems are the products of workshops and writing retreats he gives. As his students sit at laptops, lie sprawled on the floor or curled into the pillows of a sofa to write, he composes too, following the same prompts and challenges he has given them. Although he follows no single agenda, he will typically begin a session by talking about a poetic form, perhaps the villanelle or the sonnet. Sometimes he begins by reading a passage from an exotic source that he then makes relevant to the writers' own lives. Sei Shōnagon's *Pillow Book*, a record of the observations of a lady at court in Heian, Japan, first published in 1002, is a frequent choice. Musing on her lists of "splendid things" or "worthless things" or reading her description of some colorful event at court, the workshop writers are led into thinking about poems. To move to the writing, Bourque often asks them to build a word bank, usually by drawing words from the dialogue or items in a film the group watched earlier. From around the room the participants call them out: *lavender, book, shoes, blackbird.* Individually, they select six and begin their "warm-ups," short pieces in which they move the words around in different juxtapositions and contexts. There is no expectation at this point that a polished poem will emerge, just experimental lines that can be discarded later, or if a promising one appears, it may find its way into a more serious piece. After more contributions to the word bank and more warm-ups, Bourque provides a prompt, perhaps a reproduction of Albrecht Dürer's *Knight, Death, and the Devil* engraving or a photograph of one of Constantin Brancusi's *Bird in Space* works, and with his urging to make "the merely personal become the deeply personal," the serious work begins. With ample time for thinking, writing, and revising, the workshop writers compose and recompose their pieces. A read-around by those who want to share follows, concluded by Bourque's reading of his own new piece.

The popularity of the workshops and retreats, whether they are given to fourth graders or to experienced, practicing teachers, is the result of more than artful presentations, polished as they have been by Bourque's years of teaching at Northside High School in Lafayette in the early part of his career, followed by many more in classrooms at the University of Louisiana at Lafayette. The eagerness with which people return time after time to participate in the sessions he conducts is the product of something more organic. The writers and would-be writers seem to respond as much to Bourque's manner as to the information and challenges he presents. His quiet confidence is contagious, reassuring even the most inexperienced poets that the words will come. Without the use of stinging criticism or false praise, he guides, suggests, and nudges them through the process of creating poems.

Some of the most eagerly anticipated workshops are the ones Bourque holds at his home in Church Point, mostly for teachers participating in summer institutes run by Louisiana Writing Project sites. His house and the gardens that surround it are quintessential South Louisiana, with a twist. The house is actually two houses, one that he grew up in and one he had moved to his property from down the road. They are separated by a hibiscus-filled brick courtyard featuring two persimmon trees that were planted after a visit by the poet Li-Young Lee in honor of their two fathers. The houses are clearly Acadian in style, but one is painted a Caribbean peach color, and its blue shutters are a reminder of a doorway at the D. H. Lawrence ranch house in New Mexico. The sky blue of the roof echoes the island hues of the house. Inside, the houses are filled with books and art and stacks of foreign films, elements missing when Bourque lived there as a child. The gardens that surround them are the product of a year he spent studying those of Persia, leading him to replicate them by planting roses, citrus trees, and annuals. The flora grow next to outdoor sculptures in bronze and stone, and a densely planted canebrake stands on one side. Like his life and his poetry, Bourque's home both affirms his roots and honors his passions.

The genesis of some poems lies in Bourque's interaction with another work of art, a process that produces what is known as ekphrastic poetry. A case in point is *Where I Waited,* in which he takes as his springboard the paintings of Bill Gingles. Each poem is placed facing an elegantly reproduced image of the painting on which it is based. There is no attempt to replicate or describe the image in words. The challenge is to speak of what it suggests.

Whether a piece begins on a morning run or in a workshop or during meditation, turning the initial impulse into a poem involves attention to craft. In Bourque's hands, that means intense attention paid to form. His form of choice is often the sonnet, that fourteen-line lyric with a predetermined rhyme scheme. He works variations on the traditional structure, however, by grouping the lines into quatrains and three-line stanzas. By running the last line of a stanza into the first line of the succeeding one without pause, he manages to avoid the choppiness that the series of short groupings might have created, and sustains passages that sometimes sound like elegant spoken prose. Sometimes Bourque complicates the process. In the case of *Where I Waited*, for example, he chose to end the first line of each poem with the title of its paired painting. For Gingles' canvas called *When Wishing Worked,* the first line of its partner poem by Bourque reads, "I can barely remember even one time when wishing worked."

His use of language has its own pattern too. Often literal at the opening of a poem, it frequently depicts a recognizable world with edges hard and clear. As the poem develops, however, the language shifts to suggest an inner world of forces and urges that seem connected to widespread questions and answers. Just as the subject matter moves from what is local to the universal, sometimes asking questions that reach beyond the visible, questions about beginnings and endings, presence and absence, race and identity, so, too, the language itself moves to the abstract. Going beyond his depictions of the ordinary, Bourque reaches for the extraordinary.

Although a poem may begin in the mind, Bourque writes his first drafts in longhand. When he begins to revise, he turns to the computer. He explains that it allows him to pay more attention to lineage, to length and caesura and endings. On the computer screen the form of the poem emerges visually, showing where a line should carry over or end. Handwriting, he says, will let you "cheat."

Unlike some writers, he does not regularly keep a journal or record a daily set of reflections, but there are always writing materials at his elbow—a pen, a notebook, a small pad standing ready for an observation or an overheard remark. The writer self is always watching and listening because poems can hide in the smallest detail, in the most ordinary of actions. Books are always around, too, as Bourque is an avid reader not only of the work of other poets but of fiction and nonfiction. And when he is not reading or writing or teaching, he can often be found watching films—many of them foreign and exotic and thoughtful. They rarely play at your neighborhood theater.

In personal interviews he says that if he has any concerns, it is that the rich literary talent in Louisiana, like any resource, needs to be conserved and sustained. He points out that our writers are deeply committed to their art, but time and again they find it necessary to work elsewhere. He names Walter Isaacson, Yusef Komunyakaa, Martha Serpas, and Sheryl St. Germain as native talents who have had to move to universities in other states because teaching positions here are limited, and poetry alone rarely supports a family. Bourque continues to fight against that loss by supporting new writers and celebrating our established ones. He had only two years to use his position as poet laureate of Louisiana to cultivate and nurture a fragile literary system. Dedicating each day since then to that same mission, he is earning his laurel wreath. And perhaps a measure of wine.

PUBLISHED WORKS BY DARRELL BOURQUE

Plainsongs (1994)
The Doors between Us (1997)
Burnt Water Suite (1999)
The Blue Boat (2004)
Call and Response: Conversations in Verse, with Jack Bedell (2009)
In Ordinary Light: New and Selected Poems (2010)
Holding the Notes (2011)
Megan's Guitar and Other Poems (2013)
If You Abandon Me, comment je vas faire: An Amédé Ardoin Songbook (2014)
Where I Waited: Poems, with paintings by Bill Gingles (2016)

WORKS CITED

Bourque, Darrell. Personal interview, June 30, 2012.
———. Personal interview, September 8, 2015.
———. Personal interview, August 3, 2016.
———. "When Wishing Worked." *Where I Waited: Poems.* Campbell, Calif.: Yellow Flag Press, 2016.

Tim Gautreaux

Where Humor Meets Heartbreak, Always around Machinery

Tim Gautreaux claims that his goal is to write fiction that will "take readers into worlds they're discovering for the first time . . . bring them somewhere they've never been before" (Larson 2). His four short story collections and three novels do just that. They tell stories from past times, depict forgotten enterprises, and introduce eccentric characters who speak with unique accents and exhibit unusual behaviors. Although his settings, subjects, and people may strike readers as novel and surprising, they come from places and people and practices that Gautreaux knows well: his own background. As he explains, "I just weave narratives out of where I'm from" (Bauer 6).

Where he is "from" is a rich mixture of experiences, all of them potential material for his fiction. Born in Morgan City, Louisiana, he grew up with a father who was a tugboat captain, and he had a grandfather who had been a steamboat engineer. Other men in his family worked for the railroad and on offshore oil rigs. They and the machinery they introduced him to all show up in his fiction (particularly in the short stories). As a native of South Louisiana, he is a lifelong Catholic, so it is no surprise that priests appear in some of his work too.

Having done well in high school, after graduation he decided to accompany a friend who planned to go to Nicholls State University, in Thibodaux, Louisiana, making Gautreaux the first in his immediate family to go to college. (At the time, a summer semester's tuition was twenty-five dollars, and he had a scholarship that brought it down to ten dollars.) As a child, he had enjoyed writing every week to pen pals all over the world, and at Nicholls he kept on writing, turning to poetry. When one of his professors entered some of his poems in a Southern Literary Festival in Knoxville, Tennessee, James Dickey, the keynote speaker, was so impressed by them that he invited Gautreaux into the PhD program at the University of South Carolina. His dissertation was a volume of poems, "Night-Wide River."

Armed with the terminal degree, he moved on to Southeastern Louisiana University, where he would teach for thirty years. While there, he took a fiction writing class with Walker Percy at Loyola University in New Orleans and turned to writing in a new genre. His first book, a collection of short stories entitled *Same Place, Same Things*, was published in 1996, shortly before his fiftieth birthday. That year he was also invited to be the John and Renée Grisham Writer in Residence at the University of Mississippi, which gave him the opportunity to finish *The Next Step in the Dance*, his first published novel. Not surprisingly, all those years in academia make an appearance in his fiction.

Now retired, Gautreaux lives in western North Carolina, where he continues his practice of collecting odd objects from the past such as steamboat whistles, old restored lanterns, Victrolas, and even a player piano. He has steam gauges, too, one of them from a paddle wheeler. Such relics not infrequently turn up in his stories.

The fiction that emerges from the culture of his youth is populated by ordinary people, most of them white, blue-collar, South Louisiana men, many of them grandfathers. They usually operate or repair machines, and Gautreaux explains in detail the workings of their tractors and pumps and motors. As a reviewer for the *Missouri Review* pointed out, "Here is a writer who can make the refitting of an engine as compelling as another author's love or death scene" (qtd. in Bauer 2).

The lives of these men, and some women, are often marked by limited opportunities and painful setbacks, many of them of their own making. Despite disappointments, regrets, and frustrations, they appear to the reader in a surprisingly sympathetic light. Their appeal is partly due to the humor that unintentionally results from their stumbling efforts to set things right and partly because those efforts are usually attempts to make a better world, sometimes for themselves, sometimes for others.

In the short story "Welding with Children," for example, the protagonist is an occasional welder who lives in Gumwood, Louisiana, on three acres marked by an Oldsmobile engine hanging from a Kmart chain on a willow oak, a rusting truck, and various other nonworking machines scattered through clumps of pigweed. As he says, "Like any other red-dirt place in the South, trash in the yard is trash in the yard" (sec. 1).

The welder is also grandfather to and frequent babysitter for the children of four unmarried daughters. On a trip to the Pak-a-Sak, he runs into some townsmen who make disparaging remarks about his situation, and he begins to worry about the television-influenced, nonreligious environment in which his grandchildren are growing up. Fantasizing about how he can improve their circumstances, he thinks about starting over, somewhere "away from their mammas, TVs, mildew, their casino-mad grandmother, and Louisiana in general. I could get a job, raise them right, send them to college so they could own sawmills and run car dealerships." Finally, he realizes that "we couldn't drive away from ourselves" ("Welding with Children" sec. 1). All he can do is resolve to take the children to the Methodist church youth programs and clean up his yard by having the broken lawn mowers and derelict washing machines hauled away, bushhogging his three acres, and painting the house.

In Gautreaux's first novel, *The Next Step in the Dance*, the same idea of unfortunate choices followed by self-realization and attempts at self-improvement takes a different form. Paul and Colette, a young married couple with conflicting ideas about what they want out of life, are trapped by a different set of circumstances but trapped nevertheless. She longs for a richer, more glamorous life, while he is satisfied with the relaxed ambience of their Cajun village. They try to effect positive change in their surroundings by leaving family and friends to try out new lives in Los Angeles but eventually return to an economically depressed Louisiana that has suffered a downturn in the oil business. Finding that opportunities for work have disappeared, they turn to local moneymaking avenues (such as hunting nutria) in hopes of finding a way to make a living. They undergo some hair-raising swamp adventures along the way, and some laughable ones, in the end discovering that their small part of the world is where they belong. Their efforts may not have led to economic triumph, but they have led Paul and Colette to a better life together.

Their situations are not atypical of Gautreaux's people; they make bad choices and encounter hurtful circumstances yet push on in the hope of doing better, of making things better. Their efforts to deal with unfortunate experiences are admirable, but they are also often unintentionally amusing. The result is that the poignancy is balanced with humor, the painful with the laughable. It is a sympathetic view of human beings and an optimistic outlook on life. As Alan Heathcock has commented: "The stories are all about people who want to be good, who want to help others and end up helping themselves in the process. They are about redemption, with a tender sense of humor, as seen through the kind eyes of their author" (qtd. in Bauer 3).

Sometimes the efforts at improvement come from outside the troubled individual. Such is the situation in what Gautreaux calls the "intervention story," which he defines as a tale wherein "somebody's in a bad way, and a character takes that step to help, breaks through the mirror, to go to the other side. There's no story unless somebody does something like that" (Bauer 14). He calls such assistance "intervention mentality where you help people for no real reason." It is the relationship he observed growing up among his father's friends, who relied on each other to help out in times of difficulty.

In his story "The Piano Tuner," for example, the character of the title is called to an old plantation dwelling to repair a stuck note, C above middle C. The owner is a lonely thirty-something woman who is rarely seen outside of her decaying family home. It is generally assumed that she spends her days alone playing show tunes on her old upright instrument. The piano tuner is concerned by her melancholy: he "thought the saddest thing in the world was a fine instrument that nobody ever touched, so it made him uneasy that someone who could play like this lived alone and depressed in an antique nightmare of a house ten miles from the nearest ear that knew what the hell her fingers were doing" (sec. 1). Called a short time later to work again on the piano, he discovers there is nothing wrong with it. The narrator says, "He knew that when he turned around, he would have two choices: to say there was nothing wrong, get in his van, and go on with his life, or to deal with her" (sec. 3). He deals with her by helping her find a job playing the piano in a Lafayette bar. The job, along with some prescription drugs, helps alleviate her melancholy, but she is still given to outbursts of unseemly comments and actions. She commits a final irrational act when she buys herself a new piano and attempts to pull the heavy old upright out through the back door by hitching it to a John Deere tractor and in the process destroys first the back wall, then most of the rest of the house. The fire that is ignited in the kitchen takes care of what is left. The piano tuner did his best to save her, but it is questionable how effective his efforts were. The reader cannot know how successful the intervention has been.

Gautreaux's Catholicism escapes his affectionate satire no less than the bumbling welders and piano players. Clergymen, the church, and churchgoers make occasional appearances in his fiction. In "Good for the Soul," for example, Father Ledet is a well-meaning parish priest who enjoys his brandy a bit too much. While relaxing with his drink one evening, he is called to give last rites to a dying parishioner, and in a fuzzy state he has an accident on the way to the hospital. A few days later he is asked to help the dying man make restitution for a sin he committed years earlier by returning a car that he stole to its rightful owner. A second tipsy accident occurs, leading to scandal and Father Ledet's suspension from his parish duties for a short period of time. In Gautreaux's telling, it also leads to mirth.

In the glare of police headlights, the embarrassed (and guilty) clergyman tries to explain to the crowd that gathers at his arrest that he was doing a good thing, something he could not name since it had to do with a confession he had heard. "The patrolman felt sorry for him, he really did, felt bad as he filled out the tickets, as he pushed the old head under the roofline of the patrol car, and, later, as he fingerprinted the soft hands and put the holy body into the cell, taking his belt, his shoelaces, and his rosary" ("Good for the Soul" sec. 10). But it is not simply the priest whose behavior is held up for laughter. The parishioners are equally amusing. The spirituality of Clyde Arceneaux, the dying man whose confession leads to the priest's arrest, is one such example. He is not a model churchgoer by any means. "The priest had known Clyde for fifteen years. The old man dressed up on Sunday, came to church, but he stayed out on the steps and smoked with three other men as reverent as himself. As far as he knew, Clyde had never been to confession" (sec. 1).

Academia is an easy target for mockery, and Gautreaux makes good use of it. His years in higher education provided him with a rich source of material. In "Welding with Children," the grandfather-babysitter has some pithy remarks about his one semester at Louisiana State University, which he remembers as a series of puzzling experiences with professors "that don't have hearts no bigger than bird shot." The English professor is typical of the lot: "a black guy from Pakistan who couldn't understand one word we said, much less us him. He didn't teach me a damn thing and would sit on the desk with his legs crossed and tell us to write nonstop in what he called our 'portfolios,' which he never read. For all I know, he sent our tablets back to Pakistan for his relatives to use as stove wood" (sec. 1).

The Pine Oil Writers' Conference, in a story of the same name, is held at "a tiny junior college built in the shadow of an abandoned turpentine mill outside of Pine Oil, Louisiana." The school's most celebrated creative writing teacher is first seen in his black turtleneck sweater "railing against the idea that a novel had to have a plot, as though the concept were a regressive plan thought up by Republican senators." Another presenter at the conference is "a sharp-voiced stick of a woman with enormous glasses. . . . She was spare, older, wearing a denim dress and looking as tough as barbed wire. . . . [She] had published ten novels at university presses and had taught for thirty years. She had the dogged look of a classroom veteran, one of those academic martyrs long-tortured by students' outrageous questions and assumptions about writing" ("Pine Oil Writers' Conference" sec. 1). And in "Dancing with the One-Armed Gal," a one-armed professor of women's studies who claims to be a one-sixteenth African American lesbian loses her job to a black lesbian double amputee from Ghana. As she explains the situation, "The college found someone more specialized, foreign, and incomplete than I could ever be." After listening to her stories, the listener decides that "he'd rather spend eight hours a day with his tongue stuck on a hot pipe than teach in a college" (sec. 3). The satire is effective because Gautreaux's characters and episodes are so close to truth.

Gautreaux's three novels are particularly notable for taking "readers into worlds they're discovering for the first time" (Larson 2). Consequently, they bear striking similarities despite their very different subjects. They are all set in specific periods of history, all of them explore generally forgotten aspects of that time, and all involve machinery.

The Next Step in the Dance, which takes place during the oil industry downturn of the 1980s, depicts the powerfully negative impact that the economic reversal had on people's lives. In an interview with Margaret Bauer, Gautreaux explained: "I felt that if I didn't produce literature out of this, maybe nobody else would. There are lots of events in American history that are ignored and unknown because nobody wrote anything about them. . . . It's one thing to say that twenty thousand jobs were lost; it's another thing to put a reader inside the house of one of those people who lost his job" (8).

His second and third novels, *The Clearing* and *The Missing*, take place in the years just following World War I. The time period can be explained by the fact that Gautreaux had several uncles in that war, and they all came home with stories. Both Byron in *The Clearing* and Sam in *The Missing* are sent overseas, but their experiences are different. Byron, who saw fighting, returns a damaged man; Sam, who lands in France the day the armistice is signed, escapes unharmed by the war. To develop Byron, Gautreaux says he drew on the psychological damage he witnessed in an uncle who was in eight major American engagements, and Sam is defined by what he does not do.

Again, the subjects are unusual ones: *The Clearing* tells the stories of two brothers who come south to run a lumber camp in a cypress forest in Louisiana. It is a violent environment due to the natural world as well as the individuals who live and work there. The former poses threats from snakes, heat, and mosquitoes; the latter are full of menace due to whiskey, gangsters, and, not the least, Byron's damaged psyche, which sometimes causes him to move suddenly from silence to unexpected violence. *The Missing* depicts the world of excursion boats that plied the Mississippi and Ohio Rivers from around 1910 to 1940. Approximately forty or fifty such boats made stops throughout the South and the Midwest, entertaining towns along the route with jazz bands and a huge dance floor, but like the setting of *The Clearing*, nobody had written any fiction about it. Sam finds himself working on such a vessel after a little girl disappears from a department store in which he is a floorwalker, and consumed with guilt, he sets out to find her. His search takes him up and down the river, into conflict with ruffians, and into the backwoods of Arkansas and Louisiana.

Gautreaux did extensive research for both books, but his knowledge of the Mississippi River came from riding with his father, a tugboat captain, on the river. Then, too, in his youth he had ridden the Jackson Avenue Ferry and the Esplanade Avenue Ferry, reciprocating steam paddle wheel boats, just to watch the engines work. As his father knew people who worked on some of the old stern-wheel boats that were still running in the 1940s, he could go into the engine room and talk to the engineer and up to the roof to watch the pilot in the wheelhouse blow the big whistle.

The narratives of the two novels are contrasting, but the themes of moral choice, responsibility, and forgiveness run through them both. *The Clearing* explores questions of man's relation to the land, labor management, and human violence. In *The Missing*, Sam faces questions of revenge and justice, guilt and forgiveness, responsibility and blame, as he searches for the child and seeks redemption for himself. Clearly, there are serious issues at stake in both. One digression from Gautreaux's usual approach appears in *The Clearing* in that the two major characters are not southern working-class men but northerners come south. Both, however, find psychological homes in their new world, as one is empowered by the move and the other finds the isolation and anonymity he needs.

Reviewers and general readers often comment on Gautreaux's literary style. In particular, they note his ability to create characters that live and breathe with unique personalities and lifestyles. Gautreaux has also received praise for his unpretentious storytelling. It is not only accessible but inviting, with the result that his fans rarely read only one of his stories or a single novel.

It is tempting to call him a "Cajun writer" or a "southern writer," labels he objects to because, he explains, he does not set out to "ennoble or expose a culture." Nevertheless, he gets it right. His depiction of those cultures and their subcultures has authenticity that even natives recognize and approve. The characters, their language, their families, their antics, and their intentions reflect a keen ear and observant eye that make it possible for Gautreaux to reproduce incredibly accurate accents and linguistic patterns. The printed words flawlessly catch the sound and shape of real speakers. The narratives also portray the landscape of South Louisiana with uncanny accuracy. At the same time, they examine the human condition at large regardless of time or place. As a reviewer for the *North American Review* wrote, "He knows how to get out of a story's way and just let the characters do what they need to do" (qtd. in Bauer 2).

It comes as no surprise, then, that Gautreaux has been compared favorably with Flannery O'Connor and Cormac McCarthy and that he has received numerous awards and honors, including the Southern

Independent Booksellers Alliance Award for *The Clearing*, the Southeastern Booksellers Award for *The Next Step in the Dance*, the Heasley Prize, and the John Dos Passos Prize. In 2009 he received the Writer of the Year Award from the Louisiana Center for the Book in the State Library of Louisiana.

Now that Tim Gautreaux is free of the time-consuming duties of the classroom, reviewers and general readers alike are anticipating new additions to his stories and novels that have already proved to be so popular. Will his new environment take him away from steamboats, Cajuns, academia, and priests? Is he adding to "where he's from"? Regardless of where his stories are set and who populates them, they are sure to be marked by his unique mixture of humor and heartbreak, both taking place around machinery.

PUBLISHED WORKS BY TIM GAUTREAUX

Same Place, Same Things (1996)
The Next Step in the Dance (1998)
Welding with Children (1999)
The Clearing (2003)
The Missing (2009)
Waiting for the Evening News: Stories of the Deep South (2010)
Signals: New and Selected Stories (2017)

WORKS CITED

Bauer, Margaret D. "An Interview with Tim Gautreaux: 'Cartographer of Louisiana Back Roads.'" *Southern Spaces*, May 28, 2009, 1–18.

Gautreaux, Tim. "Dancing with the One-Armed Gal." *Welding with Children*. New York: Picador USA, 1999. Kindle edition.

———. "Good for the Soul." *Welding with Children*. New York: Picador USA, 1999. Kindle edition.

———. "The Piano Tuner." *Welding with Children.* New York: Picador USA, 1999. Kindle edition.

———. "The Pine Oil Writers' Conference." *Welding with Children.* New York: Picador USA, 1999. Kindle edition.

———. "Welding with Children." *Welding with Children.* New York: Picador USA, 1999. Kindle edition.

Larson, Susan. "Novelist Tim Gautreaux Is River Bound in 'The Missing.'" *New Orleans Times-Picayune*, March 11, 2009, http://blog.nola.com/susanlarson/2009/03/novelist_tim_gautreaux_is_rive.html.

Shirley Ann Grau

Maker of Myths

Shirley Ann Grau is reported to have claimed that her life has been stunningly unremarkable. "I would like just once," she said, "to have something really dramatic happen to me with trumpets and whistles and everything else, but it never really does." This from a woman who hung up on the Pulitzer Prize committee when they called to say she had won the award. "Yeah," she told the caller, "and I'm the Queen of England, too" (qtd. in Bass 1). She rode the subway to her own wedding, married a well-known Tulane philosophy professor, James Feibleman, had a cross burned on her yard by the Ku Klux Klan, published ten books of fiction and numerous short stories, and raised four children. Summers spent at Martha's Vineyard meant living with John Updike in a house on one side of her and Thornton Wilder on the other. In retrospect, it would seem to have been fairly "dramatic."

Born in New Orleans in 1929, Grau spent much of her childhood in Montgomery, Alabama. Her school years were passed in the city of her birth, as she graduated from the Ursuline Academy and attended Tulane University, where she published short stories in the university magazine. She had plans to pursue a graduate degree in literature but turned to writing fiction when the chair of the English Department, a former army major, refused to hire her as a teaching assistant because she was a woman. At that point, her interests turned to her own fiction instead of the writings of others.

Her stories and the novels to follow often reflected topics of the day that generated heated response: abortion, miscegenation, family responsibilities. She does not address them, however, through depictions of violent behavior, social upheavals, or grand events. Instead, she is concerned with the conventions and constrictions that govern society in general and the voiceless in particular. As a southerner, that inevitably means writing about race, but in Grau's case it has also meant writing about gender and power, topics that early readers often saw as the primary focus of her novels. Later readers, however, more distant from the heated controversies that swirled around the narratives at the time of their publication, are coming to see that although she was writing about topical issues of the day, many of which remain stunningly contemporary, she is also exploring larger narratives, those that approach the status of myth, stories that explain why the world is as it is and establish a rationale for social customs and observances. As she stated in a piece she wrote for *Surf,* "For me, the goal of all fiction is simply this: to make more understandable, more bearable, if you will, the muddle of human life" ("For a Place in the Sun" 7). In Grau's work, the recognition of myth is often signaled by a moment of transcendence. Such instances sometimes appear in the midst of realistic settings, thereby juxtaposing the mythopoeic and the literal. As the author pointed out early in her career, "Mythmaking is a direct route to the truth" (qtd. in Rohrberger ix).

The Keepers of the House, the novel for which she was given the Pulitzer Prize, touches on all three major subjects that recur in her writing: race, gender, and power. It is a multigenerational study of the Howlands, a powerful white family in which the patriarch secretly marries a black woman who bears him four children. Through the members of the family, their servants, and townspeople, Grau examines the complex relationships of whites and blacks, racial hypocrisy, the limiting roles of women, and the struggles between the powerful and the powerless, the affluent and the poor. It is not too much to say that the Howland family saga is a microcosm of the South, its history and its culture.

Published at the height of the civil rights movement, *The Keep-*

ers of the House was not well received by some. Grau was attacked by people on both sides of the desegregation issue, by both blacks and whites. Some white critics wondered about the authenticity of a white writer telling a story that belongs to African Americans. On the other hand, anti-integrationists burned a cross on her Metairie lawn when she was out of town. (She was not criticized for assuming the voice of a black woman in this narrative, but she would be later when she published *Roadwalkers.*)

Although *The Keepers of the House* is easily read as a novel about racism and political power, with time its larger dimensions have also become apparent. Today's reader is likely to see that its characters exude mythlike qualities that extend their significance beyond a specific time and place. In the section entitled "William," for example, William, the patriarch, goes on a heroic quest through Honey Island Swamp to find a hidden moonshine still. The swamp is a place of mystery that he challenges in his search: "It began abruptly in a sharp dip of the sandy ground, a wide irregular stretch of swamp—of river birch and water oak, of black gum and dahoon bushes grown into full-sized trees. And cypress, mile after mile of dreary moss-hung cypress and oily thick water. Boys played around its margins, crawfishing in the spring, gigging frogs at night, chasing the big sirens, the eel-like animals that flashed along the water. But nobody dared go very far inside."

While on his quest, he first sees Margaret, the black woman who will become his wife, through a fog, making her appear to him as a vision: "His eyes circled the pool twice before he saw the woman. She was that earth-colored. She knelt at the side of the creek, just above the baptistery, washing clothes. Her dress was brown, her hair black as her skin. Only a flash of bright yellow from the material in her hand caught William's eye. In the sudden noise of fighting mockingbirds the sounds of her splashing disappeared. William wondered for a minute if she were really there at all—if, soundless, she wasn't a part of the morning fog that twisted between the trees behind her."

Later they live in a world set apart for themselves, protected by secrecy that shields them from the ordinary and conventional rituals of their day. Some critics have noted that they become an Adam and Eve attempting to create a new Eden. As the author once commented to her friend Mary Rohrberger, *The Keepers of the House* "is not about race so much as it is about good and evil and the interactions among people that can have disastrous results despite their good intentions" (qtd. in Rohrberger 181).

Gender issues appear in much of Grau's fiction, but they are perhaps most directly addressed in *The House on Coliseum Street*, a novel published in 1961, a time of ferment on many fronts, one of them caused by feminist calls for change. In the novel, Joan, a young woman who has recently had an abortion, tries to find her way in a society ruled by class and conventions that hold women to a limited role, at least as publicly perceived. She has tried to conform to her mother's wishes that she marry an acceptable but boring young man. As a contrast to his tiresome propriety, she has a fling with a college professor, the affair that leads to the abortion. After returning to college, a less than gratifying experience, she reconnects with the professor, only to be betrayed and humiliated by him. In the end she finds herself on the doorstep of her family home, locked out and alone, having accomplished only one thing: the professional destruction of the offending professor-lover. Unable to cope with the world in which she finds herself, she grows increasingly deranged and obsessed, and the novel ends without any foreseeable future for her. As in many of Grau's novels, there is no denouement, no closure, no tidy wrap-up of conflicts and relationships. Joan is not at peace with her world, nor has she found her place in it.

Surrounding the narrative of Joan's discontent is a wider one of family continuity in which she is caught. The house itself is home not just to Joan, her sisters, and her mother, but to all who have preceded them. Joan perceives it in its smell: "It was the smell of everything. Of everything that had gone on in the house for the past hundred and twenty years. It was the smell of the people and the things. Of the living that had gone on between the walls. The smell of generations being born. Dying. And being laid out in the front parlor with a sprig of sweet olive from the door in their clenched hand" (Grau, *House* pt. 4, "Winter"). At such a moment, Joan sees herself not as an individual living at a particular time but as a member of a chain of living beings. She recognizes that she belongs to a larger story than her own; she is part of a mythos that has shaped her life.

A different way of looking at gender issues is apparent in the several strong, independent women who populate Grau's fiction. They do not sit on pedestals. *Roadwalkers*, for example, tells the story of two women, an African American mother and daughter, who over the years rise from poverty to affluence, from invisibility to public status, from darkness to light. Rohrberger asserts that through Mary, the mother, the novel traces the journey "from the beginnings of civilization to contemporary western culture reflected through the experiences of a black child who grows up and eventually prospers" (287).

Mary and Nanda, her daughter, are strong women who face down the odds of survival and success. Their strength comes from the myths they weave for themselves. Mary, whose early years are spent as a speechless child, by force of will and strength goes on to establish an upscale clothing line while she raises Nanda to believe she is an exotic princess living in an enchanted castle. "You are," she would say, "the queen of the world, the jewel of the lotus, the pearl without price, my secret treasure." With little contact outside her mother's world except for attending an all-white—except for her—girls' school, she accepts her exotic, if fictive, inheritance. Eventually, Nanda finds herself in a world of sophisticated weariness, and she is sustained by the myth that her mother wove around her as a child. She says: "When the kingdom finally fell and the castle was conquered, and I lost my crown and my birthright, when I stood naked and revealed as a young black female of illegitimate birth, it hardly mattered. By then the castle and the kingdom were within me and I carried them away" (Grau, "Magic Kingdom").

The myth has softened the hard edges of reality for Nanda. She later recalls the magical realm of their own making, saying: "We built two kingdoms, she [Mary] and I. One of walled gardens where roses bloomed all year and gold carp swam in marble lily pools, where she was queen and I was princess, where our castle gates were guarded by the flaming swords of cherubim. Through all our ordinary days my mother and I carried this gleaming private world with us, hermit crabs, walking ponderously, and castles on our backs, secure." Nanda also recalls another world: "Our second kingdom, a kind of distant shadow of the first, was strong and firm and enduring in the human world, rooted in reality, based on money and prosperity and the logic of commerce. Its treasures were measured by bank accounts and corporate statements" ("Magic Kingdom").

Nanda grows up in both worlds, the experiential and the mythic. She recognizes that her mother is a "woman of flickering eyes, setting traps for dollars." She is also "a sorceress of spells and illusions." In the lives of the two women the real and the mythopoeic are juxtaposed.

Power is on naked display in several of Grau's novels but never more than in *The Condor Passes.* Central to the novel is Thomas Henry Oliver, who as a young man would do anything, legal or illegal, to make money that would give him power. As an old man, he has grown to physically resemble a vulture that spends its waning years in a greenhouse watching a trap that holds live birds. The fascination with money and power has left him with a harsh, condor-like cough, clawlike hands, and a bald head atop his tall, thin body. Poisoned by his thirst for wealth, which he equates with power, he has come to represent death itself. Even Stanley, Oliver's faithful manservant, to whom he leaves a fortune, shows traces of a similar lust, and the novel ends inconclusively, as usual, as the reader does not learn what Stanley will do with his new fortune.

The overarching myth, in the case of *The Condor Passes,* is so close to the literal truth that it is hard to see it for itself. It is the story of the consequences of being willing to do anything to acquire wealth and power. The cost of avaricious desires and the means required to serve them is death in life. The connection between Thomas Henry

Oliver, the condor, and the national bird, the American eagle, cannot be missed, making Oliver's life an indictment of a warped version of the American dream.

Love is ostensibly the focus of *Evidence of Love*, and indeed the novel does explore several of the varied forms it can take, but the desire for and uses of power are also a part of the narrative. For example, Edward Milton Henley, another of Grau's powerful male characters, equates money and the power it bestows with love. He buys love from mistresses and attempts to do so with his son and daughter-in-law. Like his father before him, who sent strawberries to comfort his wife when she was in labor instead of attending her in person, Henley exercises his wealth to make the world conform to his wishes. He rejects the mythos of his "proper" parents, who live by a strict social code that has clearly defined rituals and behaviors, and adopts instead one of Dionysian dimensions that allow him to explore the dark underside of life. The stance is underscored by frequent classical allusions—for example, references to Virgil's metaphor of choppy waters, which become racing white horses forever "yoked into chariot teams," and Henley's mention of Clotho, Agapos, and Atropos, the Three Fates. Henley even seems to imitate a Greek god visiting earth to sire a child by an unknown woman when he hires a stranger to bear his son.

All of these major topics—race, gender identity, and power—and the myths that surround them are straining between stasis and change in the fiction of Shirley Ann Grau. The strain is evident as racial relationships are questioned, women push to move from social conformity to an authentic identity, and the powerful in society give way, albeit reluctantly, to the powerless, if only by death. In each case the known is more comfortable than the unfolding and unknown, but it can also be stultifying and limiting, putting the two forces in tension with each other.

Change is sometimes a matter of choice, sometimes of force. It is never implemented without resistance. In Grau's novels, the resistance to social modification is suggested by the recurring image of a house, which suggests continuity, stability, and ordered routine. (Note that the word *house* appears in the titles of two of the novels.) The houses that frequent her novels provide a sense of the enduring past and the traditions that compose the myth of family. They give the present a firm sense of place. As noted earlier, in *The House on Coliseum Street* Joan recognizes her house as having been composed of generations past that made the present possible. In *The Keepers of the House,* the remaining member of the family fights to protect it as the locus of the family's history. In *The Condor Passes,* Anna asks her father to buy her a house in New Orleans before she is sixteen years old and proceeds to remodel it. On her honeymoon she falls in love with an old hotel, which she also asks for and subsequently works to restore. In her case, "home" provides fulfillment for her that she does not find elsewhere.

The sense of belonging, the antidote to the uncertainties of change, is also firmly established by Shirley Ann Grau's power to create a sense of place by her detailed descriptions of the natural world. She exhibits an astounding knowledge of flora and fauna and the animal world, a trait clearly exhibited in her first novel, *The Hard Blue Sky.* Set on a small island in the Gulf of Mexico, it tells the story of an unruly population that is dependent on nature for its sustenance. The people who live there are almost as wild as the packs of dogs that roam free on the island and the dangerous labyrinths of the swamp that surround it. Grau's detailed depiction of that natural world and the natives' identification with it is both lyrical and revealing of their acceptance of life as it is. Describing Isle aux Chiens, named for its wild dogs, in the opening chapter, "The White Afternoon," the narrator says:

> The rest of the island has nothing but oaks, their trunks and branches twisted by the wind and the spray; oleanders with branches thick as a man's arm, and covered with pink and white and red flowers in the spring and summer—only, their smooth, dark pointed leaves are poison. Hibiscus and

> its midsummer flowers. Wisteria and bougainvillea so thick you have to cut your way through. Chinaberry trees with their tiny whitish purple flowers in March—and the stifling rotting smell of the yellow berries on the ground in December. And in the marshy spots, reeds that rustle and crackle their hollow stems together in the slightest wind, canes six feet high or more in patches where stones say there were painters once.

Weather, on the other hand, plays a significant role in revealing characters' desire for change and fear of its consequences. *The Hard Blue Sky* ends with a hurricane that equals the fury and chaos of the islanders themselves. *The House on Coliseum Street* opens with the approach of a storm from off the Gulf, catching Joan playing cards in an open gazebo, unmistakably foreshadowing her turbulent life to come. And the sky, "like a teacup fitted overhead, close and hard and shiny as china" (chap.1), is a frequent figure that appears in more than one novel.

The olfactory sense is at play as well, with characters sensing the power of the past and the meaning of the present through the smells they encounter. Joan's moment of recognition of her family's history through the smells of the house is not the only such experience. In the section entitled "The Secret Thief" in *The Condor Passes,* for example, Stanley's attitude toward the greenhouse in which he sits with the dying Thomas Henry Oliver is apparent in his objection to "its heavy sweet flower smells, its dripping perfumes and masks. Reminded him of funerals." Earlier, in a section entitled "The Old Man," an ugly incident in Oliver's youth takes place on a houseboat where "the odor of whiskey hung faintly in the room, mixing with the sour smell of the Ohio."

Grau's use of elements outside of the characters to reveal their frustrations with the status quo and their accompanying fears of losing it is not surprising. The dense network of symbols that lie beneath any of the plots works to develop the overarching myths that create and sustain the characters of all the novels. There are the stuffed owls

Joan's lover searches for in *The House on Coliseum Street*, just as dead and hollow as he is. There are the 9,653 books that Stephen prizes in *Evidence of Love*, a collection that supersedes any love he has for his wife. There is the greenhouse in which Thomas Henry Oliver spends his days, an environment of imprisonment and death.

Shirley Ann Grau, as a writer who seeks to sort out what she calls "the muddle of life," is inevitably drawn to physical objects and natural elements as manifestations of myths that support conventional attitudes and daily behavior. As she once said to Mary Rohrberger, "Reality does not carry meaning in itself; writers must push their way through a world of fact into a world of meaning" (217).

And so she does.

PUBLISHED WORKS BY SHIRLEY ANN GRAU

NOVELS

The Hard Blue Sky (1959)
The House on Coliseum Street (1961)
The Keepers of the House (1964)
The Condor Passes (1972)
Evidence of Love (1977)
Roadwalkers (1994)

SHORT STORIES

The Black Prince and Other Stories (1955)
The Wind Shifting West (1973)
Nine Women (1986)
Selected Stories (2003)

UNCOLLECTED SHORT STORIES

"The Things You Keep," in *Carnival* (1950)
"The Fragile Age," in *Carnival* (1951)
"The Beginning of Summer," in *Story* (1961)
"The First Day of School," in *Saturday Evening Post* (1961)
"The Empty Night," in *Atlantic* (1962)
"The Loveliest Day," in *Saturday Evening Post* (1962)
"On Night," in *Gentlemen's Quarterly* (1966)

WORKS CITED

Bass, Erin Z. "The Undramatic Life of Shirley Ann Grau." *Deep South Magazine,* October 13, 2013, deepsouthmag.com/2013/10.31/the-undramatic-life-of-shirley-ann-grau/.

Grau, Shirley Ann. *The Condor Passes.* New York: Open Road Integrated Media, n.d. Kindle edition.

———. "For a Place in the Sun." *Surf* (1948): 7.

———. *The Hard Blue Sky.* New York: Open Road Integrated Media, n.d. Kindle edition.

———. *The House on Coliseum Street.* New York: Open Road Integrated Media, n.d. Kindle edition.

———. *The Keepers of the House.* New York: Open Road Integrated Media, n.d. Kindle edition.

———. *Roadwalkers.* New York: Open Road Integrated Media, n.d. Kindle edition.

Rohrberger, Mary. "Too Silver for a Seam: The Fiction of Shirley Ann Grau." MS, n.d.

Greg Guirard

A Life on Bayou Amy

In July 1845, Henry David Thoreau moved from Concord, Massachusetts, to a small cabin near Walden Pond, where he resolved to "live deliberately, to front only the essential facts of life, and see if I could not learn what it had to teach, and not, when I came to die, discover that I had not lived." More than a century later and many miles farther south, Greg Guirard, in a similar search for serenity and meaning, moved to a wooden cottage on Bayou Amy outside of Henderson, Louisiana. As Guirard comments in *Atchafalaya Autumn II:* "I think to live deliberately, as Thoreau meant it, must be to do something, on a regular basis, that allows a person to experience his senses consciously, and somehow slowly. . . . The opposite of deliberately is mechanically. I do not want to live mechanically, superficially" (52). In the end, what began as a personal quest for change within himself led Guirard to develop a deep concern for changes in the natural world and his own culture. He deals with his unease—personal, natural, and cultural—by publishing books and photographs of uncommon beauty and power that testify to the increasingly strong connection he has to the land of his birth and to his culture. They reflect the evolution of his search for tranquility, his respect for the natural world, and his fierce desire to protect it.

Early on, Guirard had no plans to make his life in the Atchafalaya Basin. It took him some time to realize his place and purpose. In fact, he himself says he has spent most of his life looking for his proper direction. He refers to the condition as "DDD," or "direction-deficit-disorder." Growing up near the West Atchafalaya Basin Protection Levee, as a boy of eleven or twelve he would accompany his grandfather, Wade O. Martin Jr., who served as Louisiana's secretary of state under five governors from 1944 to 1976, on hunting trips in the Basin, but as a young man, he had little connection with it. At the University of Southwestern Louisiana (USL, now the University of Louisiana at Lafayette), he tried out majors in geology and chemical engineering, then moved to Louisiana State University (LSU), where he studied forestry, oceanography, and agriculture, eventually earning a degree in agronomy. (He graduated from LSU with the highest number of credit hours anyone had accrued up to that time.) Discovering a love of literature, Guirard moved on to graduate school, where he turned his attention to English and American literature. He wrote his thesis on William Faulkner, and when he read *The Bear,* he connected with the wilderness in which it is set in a powerful and lasting way. (The pull the story exerted on him is evident in his habit of rereading it every November.) Despite the lure to live a less hurried, more focused life, for a time he continued to work outside of the world that he would belong to later, serving as a university English instructor, a farmer and cattleman, and a sawmill worker. Since realizing that his cultural and personal home is in the Atchafalaya Basin, he has been, in addition to a photographer and writer, a carpenter and furniture maker, a crew boat driver, a crawfisherman, and an actor and technical advisor to film production companies. He is, it would seem, more complex than his lifestyle suggests.

When he decided to "simplify" his life by leaving his university teaching position and returning to his roots, Guirard turned to two passions that still connect him to the natural world: collecting wood and crawfishing. As the stacks of driftwood and sinkers, old cypress logs lost years ago by lumber harvesters—or "swampers," as they were called—piled up on his property, he began to slice some of them into slender sections that revealed their growth rings and patterns; others he turned into lumber and furniture. His home today is ornamented with pieces large and small hanging on the walls and serving as benches and tables. By 1993 he was selling cypress to plant nurseries and other buyers, but on occasion he would discover a piece too beautiful to relinquish. Recently finding himself unable to bring himself to sell one particularly lovely curved piece, he agreed to lease it to the would-be buyer. To celebrate its beauty, they called it the "Big Curly Madonna."

Guirard came by his second passion, crawfishing, almost by accident but says that today he would do it for a living—if it provided a living. In it he finds the satisfaction of being involved in a traditional Cajun vocation, a satisfaction that is perhaps more significant than the financial rewards it produces. He may be the only crawfisherman who chooses his fishing places on the basis of how beautiful they are. He is surely the only one who breaks his labor by stopping at noon to read a novel while eating lunch.

Guirard's search for a more focused life intensified a few years ago when he decided that his attempts to "simplify, simplify, simplify" were not enough. He determined that he would just drop out, quit doing what he was supposed to do, and instead live on his houseboat, create cypress pieces, take pictures, and read. The solitude was gratifying, but ultimately one night he recanted to attend a meeting of crawfishermen where Dean Wilson, Atchafalaya Basinkeeper, was to speak. Wilson's information about the Basin's problems and his ideas about how to restore it to some kind of health resonated with Guirard, evoking a sense of activism. What he heard that night led him to believe it was up to the people who love the area and depend on it for their livelihoods to make it viable again. The problems are many and serious.

For one, invasive plant species, many of them brought here with the approval of the U.S. government, are clogging countless waterways. So massive is the proliferation of water hyacinths, hydrilla, salvinia, and more that canoeing in late spring and summer is nearly impossible now. They are so numerous that they choke themselves, rot, and deplete the water of oxygen. Another problem is that the Army Corps of Engineers, in charge of flood control, purposely directs over

30 percent of water from the Mississippi River and over 60 percent of the sediment load into the Atchafalaya, raising the possibility that the southern part of the Basin will fill up. Its swamps once reached to Simmesport, Louisiana, but today the northern part is farmland, and the remaining cypress-tupelo swamps are disappearing under load after load of Mississippi River sediments. Guirard's writing and photography are powerful means for him to voice his concern that the Basin is gradually becoming less and less productive, its beauty is being destroyed, and a sizable portion of the Cajun community can no longer practice the livelihoods they have traditionally followed there.

Guirard says that the flood of 2011 was expected to be both a blessing and a curse. The optimistic view was that it would clean up the Basin by killing and washing away some of the invasive plants. It should have replaced water that had become stagnant (because canals and spoil banks had blocked flowing currents) with oxygen-rich water that would boost the fish and crawfish populations. Birds were expected to benefit from the increase of fish, and new wetlands should have been created as the Delta grew. Even the cypress and tupelo trees should have grown healthier due to the nutrient-rich sediment it would provide. The negative view was that added sediments would mean losing more of the inland forested wetlands and decreasing the depth of bayous and lakes, affecting their health as aquatic habitats. Animals such as deer, rabbits, and armadillos would be threatened. Especially disturbing was the fact that the flood was expected to arrive during the breeding season for birds, meaning that some species already in decline would be affected.

In actuality, it seems that only the bad news happened. The banner crawfish season that the added water should have produced never materialized. For reasons that Guirard says no one understands, the yield did not improve as it did during the floods in 1973 and 1983. In those good years everyone was busy every day. In fact, the crawfish were so plentiful that in 1984 the fishermen, led by Guirard, organized a cooperative so they could work for themselves rather than for the buyer-processors and thereby receive a fair price for their crawfish. In contrast, in later years fishermen found themselves busy only a day or two a week because of decreases in the yield. Even experienced crawfishermen found themselves in trouble, and young people could not afford the cost of equipping themselves to enter the business with no good reason to think they could succeed. The bad news did not end there. As expected, millions of tons of new sediment were fed into the Atchafalaya Basin from the river, further filling the swamps and bayous with sand and silt.

It has not only been the dwindling crawfish yields that affect those working in the Basin. Guirard points out that other traditional livelihoods are equally imperiled. Gone are the days when a person could support a family by trapping, cutting cypress, picking moss, hunting alligators, and fishing. The lack of demand for furs has made trapping unprofitable. Catfishing used to go on year-round, but as is the case for crawfish and even alligators, most of the market is now supplied by farms. Occasionally, extra money can be made by conducting swamp tours for visitors, but tourism has had little effect on the area so far. Most people take a short boat ride and don't experience "the real Basin," Guirard says, "where you have to have a boat and know where you are" (personal interview). That may be a good thing, he adds, since too many people would destroy the solitary feeling of the swamps. The bottom line is that the age-old ways of making a living are disappearing. Despite its dwindling rewards, crawfishing is the only thing left for Cajuns living near the Basin, he says.

Guirard's commitment to helping implement the ideas that Dean Wilson put forth at the meeting of crawfishermen he attended ended his renunciation of the larger world. He was put on the board of Atchafalaya Basinkeeper, an organization dedicated to protecting and restoring the ecosystems within the Atchafalaya Basin. It works to protect the area's long-term health and sustainability, supports public access to any place in the Basin that one can go by boat, recognizes the need to improve water quality and limit sedimentation, and tries to protect the rights of crawfishermen. With little help coming from the state or the federal government, the only hope for saving the Basin, according to Guirard, is for the people who love it and work in it to protect it.

One reason Guirard has such passion for the Basin and the crawfishing that goes on there is that he sees it as virtually synonymous with Cajun culture, so much of which, he feels, has been diluted and taken over by the rest of the world. He points out that Cajun restaurants serve faux dishes in cities across the country and that Mardi Gras is now celebrated by people who never heard "Throw me something, Mister" until a few years ago. Cajun French is used mostly by older people since the young have grown up with English only. In his view, all that is left untouched and undistorted are crawfishing and the Cajun French of fishermen talking to each other as they make a living by practicing the traditional occupations of their culture. Guirard sees beauty in their labor: they preserve the past as they carry on their work in a unique and lovely environment. He keeps them alive in his written and photographed records of them, such as those found in *Atchafalaya Autumn II.*

The spread of Cajun culture beyond the borders of Acadiana has led Guirard to refer to the adaptations and distortions as "Cajun Theme Parks" because, he says, they are not genuine. What is genuine about the Basin, he says, are the people. In his books he shows that they expect to work hard and to be self-sufficient and that they like it that way. He argues that most are generous and quick to help someone in need. They exhibit a gentleness and respect for older people not always seen in other places. He admires their spirit, their love of existence, their excitement about life. For example, like others in the Basin who seem to thrive on hard work, his friend Roy Blanchard and his wife, Annie, who figure in Guirard's writing about the area, fish and work together, and about 75 percent of what they eat is something they have caught or hunted.

Guirard's resistance to change in the Basin and his passion for maintaining the way of life that exists in it stem from the beauty he discovered there as he saw it with the eyes of a photographer. Troubled by misconceptions that people have of the Basin—their assumption that the swamps are ugly and sinister—he began publishing his photographs and stories to show them the beauty he finds in it and thereby shape their attitudes toward it. He wants others to know that the area is not a steamy, snake-infested, mosquito-ridden place but one of serenity, beauty, and peace. He champions that cause at every opportunity. In June 2011, for example, he introduced the television public to the Basin he knows so well during an appearance on the "America the Beautiful" segment of NBC's *Today Show* in an interview by Jenna Bush Hager.

Looking back, he comments, "I never saw myself as a photographer or a writer" (personal interview). At the age of twelve, however, he began asking his grandfather to let him use his old fold-out Kodak to record the world around him. His interest in photography was revived years later when Jeff Caffery, a student Guirard taught at USL and later a close friend, gave him a camera. He began using photography seriously around 1972 to document the changes he observed in his world. Learning by trial and error the art and craft involved, after ten years he felt he had a sufficient number of images to compose a book. When he approached a local press about publishing it, he was told that another photographer from the area, who had just published a book of Atchafalaya photos, had exhausted the market. Guirard's response to the rejection would become a lifelong pattern: he took out a hefty loan from the bank to self-publish *Seasons of Light in the Atchafalaya Basin.* Its robust sales left him in the black, giving him sufficient encouragement to publish *Cajun Families of the Atchafalaya* five years later. Again coupling vivid photographs with a prose text, he documented the lives of Cajuns who earn their livelihood by fishing, trapping, crabbing, and hunting in the Basin. The book depicts their struggles and dreams, their attitudes and family life.

As he found success with his photographs, the texts he wrote to accompany them led him to realize that he had something to say, and he has now been saying it for over twenty-five years. Together the words and pictures capture the lives of a people at a particular time and in a special place. He calls his books "Cajun documentaries." By telling the stories of a culture and the land it is bound to, both what it was and what it has become, he calls attention to the beauty of the natural world and humankind's obligation to honor it.

Guirard's treatment of these subjects cannot be described as traditional or even systematic. The order of the stories he tells and the photographs of the people in them reflect his own moods and interests. Consequently, he continues to self-publish because by doing so he is not restricted by editors or layout designers. He can profile the people who interest him in the order he wants to present them. He can indulge his love of sunrises and sunsets as subjects for photographs, repeatedly recording those moments when the vibrant colors of the sky are reflected in the water, enveloping the viewer in a flamboyant glow.

An example of the nontraditional presentation of his books is his insertion of French from time to time. Sometimes he makes a remark or two in Cajun French, and in at least one book, *The Land of Dead Giants,* he repeats the entire text in standard French. (He speaks both.) Other surprising inclusions are recipes for turtle sauce picante, garfish patties, and baked gaspergou with tomato sauce, which are presented with some frequency. (Guirard learned to cook from Junice Savoy, who stirred the pots in his grandfather's deer hunting camp, a large, dilapidated building located, he recalls, on a high Indian mound. When Junice died, out of respect for his culinary and hunting skills, the family laid him out in his hunting clothes with a shotgun propped against the casket.) Sometimes Guirard includes writings by other people in his books—for example, Sheryl St. Germain has two pieces in *Psychotherapy for Cajuns,* and *Seasons of Light* carries two short stories by William Faulkner. And when he is not reprinting entire poems or essays by someone else, he peppers his writing with quotations from William Faulkner, Ernest Hemingway, Siddhartha, Henry David Thoreau, Mark Twain, and William Wordsworth, along with references to classical music and comments about what he has heard on National Public Radio. When such allusions appear in a passage discussing the use of hoop nets to catch garfish and buffalo fish, the result is a unique mixture of sophistication and simplicity. Like the man himself, his writing combines a respect for things of the earth and things of the mind.

The book that deviates from the documentary style is *The Land of Dead Giants*. In this piece of short fiction, the story of Aristile Guilbeau and his Cajun family depicts what it was like to live off the land in the Basin in 1948. Ti Frere lives with his mother and grandfather, along with a milk cow and a few chickens, ducks, and geese, in "a one-story unpainted cypress house surrounded by a picket fence made of hand-split cypress." When they speak, the language is often nonstandard but authentic. To read the dialogue out loud is to hear the Cajun accent and dialect reproduced with uncanny fidelity. Ti Frere explores the surrounding swamps in his pirogue, learns to love the mysterious world in which he lives, and tries to understand how, in the late 1800s and early 1900s, men could have cut down all of the gigantic cypress trees that once grew there. The forest of big trees was destroyed for lumber, and Ti Frere knows that it cannot be replaced in his lifetime. Though the narrative reads like a fable, *The Land of Dead Giants* is a serious indictment of the destruction of nature for private gain. It has been made into a stage play as well as a screenplay.

Guirard's most recent books, *Inherit the Atchafalaya*, written with C. Ray Brassieur, and *Atchafalaya Autumn II*, are complementary volumes. The former covers the cultural history and folklife of the Basin, along with interviews and comments that accompany photographs. The latter is Guirard's attempt to record the essence of the place and its people in times of change. They are handsome books as well as serious commentaries.

A quiet sadness runs through all of Guirard's reflections on the world he writes about, a yearning for what once was, regret for what has been lost—the language, the livelihoods, the cypress forest. Although he recognizes that change is inevitable, he laments that its appearance means that some assurances of the past no longer hold. He points out that in earlier times property left outside was safe, but things disappear now, and wanton acts of destruction and theft are not uncommon. People steal traps and throw trash in pristine spaces. "Changes like that," he says, "hurt." They impair the beauty of a way of life that allows people to make a living off the land. Such acts give him grave concern for what he calls in *Atchafalaya Autumn II* "the welfare of the human spirit" (10). That is, when ugly things happen, the sunrises and sunsets may still be glorious, but the loveliness of life is marred. Sounding a little like Huckleberry Finn, he says, "I wish people were better" (personal interview).

Asked about his current writing projects, he initially demurs, saying, "I don't really know I'm going to write a book until it hits me in the face" (personal interview). Later he speculates that it might be time to revisit the individuals and families featured in his 1989 *Cajun Families of the Atchafalaya*, looking to see what has happened to them and their lives over the past decades. If he does, you can be sure he will be acutely aware of the changes that have come to the people and their place.

In the meantime, Guirard continues to collect his cypress, check his crawfish traps, photograph sunrises and sunsets in the swamp, write his books, and search for peace of mind on Bayou Amy. Explaining his efforts, he says: "I look to Thoreau for encouragement in this work, this approach to life. Sometimes I speak to him. 'Henry David,' I say aloud, 'I'm tryin' to simplify, but it's not easy'" (personal interview).

PUBLISHED WORKS BY GREG GUIRARD

Seasons of Light in the Atchafalaya Basin (1983)
Cajun Families of the Atchafalaya (1989)
The Land of Dead Giants (1991)

Atchafalaya Autumn (1995)
Psychotherapy for Cajuns (2006)
Inherit the Atchafalaya, with C. Ray Brassieur (2007)
Atchafalaya Autumn II (2010)

WORKS CITED

Guirard, Greg. *Atchafalaya Autumn II*. Published by the author, 2010.

———. Personal interview, July 14, 2013.

Thoreau, Henry David. "Where I Lived, and What I Lived For." *Walden*. Reprint of the 1845 edition, *The Thoreau Reader: Annotated Works by Henry David Thoreau*, 2016, thoreau.eserver.org/walden02.html.

William Joyce

Guardian of Childhood

To understand pretending is to conquer all barriers of time and space.
—*Nicholas St. North and the Battle of the Nightmare King*

Walking into William Joyce's Moonbot Studios is like walking into one of his books. Entirely inviting and comfortable, it nevertheless produces a sense of having stumbled across life in another dimension, one that is whimsical but serious, collegial but private, one that crackles with energy and ideas while it is hushed and quiet.

Located in what was planned to be a Bio-Tech Research Park in Shreveport, Louisiana, the studio was redesigned on the interior to reflect its personality. After threading one's way through enough security to conjure up the CIA, the visitor opens heavy glass doors to enter a slightly futuristic environment gleaming with glass and chrome. A receptionist sits behind a curved desk under a suspended oversized lamp that is perhaps ten feet in diameter. It appears to be activated by a "pull chain" of wooden balls. (In actuality one turns it on by flicking a switch on the wall.) A lighted case exhibits four Emmys, a gold medal from the Society of Illustrators, fourteen Cannes Lions, twelve Clios, and five Webbys that Moonbot has earned, including the Oscar that Joyce and his partner, Brandon Oldenburg, won in 2012 for the animated film *The Fantastic Flying Books of Mr. Morris Lessmore.* The chairs are deep and multihued, some of them mounted like lazy Susans that revolve, and above, exposed pipes gleam in foil wrapping. Bold, primary colors are everywhere.

On either side of the hall leading from the foyer are rooms housing work pods specially designed to give people space and privacy without putting them out of touch with each other. Books are stacked high on desks and tables, while illustrations from *The Leaf Men*, *Dinosaur Bob*, and other Joyce books and films hang on the walls and sit on the floor propped against them. Office whiteboards are crowded with lists of projects, deadlines, and assignments; storyboards charting Moonbot's projects in progress cover the walls of two large rooms. At the end of the corridor is a screening room where the staff can examine the craft of moviemaking (as in Buster Keaton's films, *Singin' in the Rain*, and others) and review their own projects. Oversized red beanbags that spill across the floor seem to be the seats of choice.

In short, the ambience of Moonbot Studios, like the books and films Moonbot produces, is surprising, imaginative, engaging. The "Bots" (the studio's young, energetic, talented employees) have taken a work space and turned it into a creative area that combines innovative uses of technology with the best of artistic imagination. The result is an electric atmosphere that pulsates with energy, a little eccentric perhaps but simultaneously engaging and challenging.

At the heart of all this is William Joyce, a bespectacled artist in his midfifties whose seriousness about visual storytelling is betrayed on occasion by a sense of mischief. For his attendance at the Academy Awards, for example, he, along with Oldenburg, wore a tuxedo made by Dickies Workwear. Joyce added a hat to his ensemble. On any ordinary day, however, he can typically be seen in white jeans and a tieless shirt with the sleeves rolled up, his small beard and mustache neatly trimmed, and his graying hair cropped short. On occasion he wears a white lab coat that is similar to a doctor's office jacket, only Joyce's sports a small blue logo that resembles some of his characters. He is neither short nor tall, neither attention catching nor invisible. Where the atmosphere of Moonbot Studios is inventive, ingenious, and original, fairly shouting its creative qualities, to outsiders Joyce himself gives few external clues about what must be going on inside.

Those inner impulses to create art came naturally. Joyce knew early on that he was meant to draw. Even today Ann Jacobs, one of his art teachers, remembers that his talent was evident in childhood. As a preschooler in the late 1950s, he was struck by the illustrations he found in Maurice Sendak's *Where the Wild Things Are*, and in the fourth grade, at A. C. Steere Elementary School in Shreveport, he produced his first book. By the time he was in Byrd High School, he was drawing cartoons for *High Life*, the school's newspaper. When his post–high school art instructors urged him to change his style, he decided to study film, graduating with a bachelor of fine arts degree from Southern Methodist University. It turned out to be good training for a visual storyteller.

After college Joyce tried being an artist in New York, but when one of the dealers to whom he was showing his portfolio remarked that he could do what he did anywhere, he returned to his hometown of Shreveport and stayed. He liked being around people he knew, and the burgeoning film industry that was growing there was attractive. Although success was not immediate, his creative impulses just kept coming. "If you really love to write," he says, "and you really love to draw, you just have to keep doing it no matter what anybody says" (personal interview).

He did "keep doing it," and by the mid-1980s the reading public had begun to take notice of the whimsical tales and lush illustrations found in books such as *George Shrinks* and *Dinosaur Bob and His Adventures with the Family Lazardo*. The 1990s saw even more productivity, including *A Day with Wilbur Robinson*, based, according to Joyce, on his own family; *Santa Calls* (set partly in Abilene, Texas, which caused the city to establish the National Center for Children's Illustrated Literature there); and *Rolie Polie Olie* (introducing a character destined in the next decade to star in *Snowie Rolie, Big Time Olie*, and *Sleepy Time Olie*).

Several of his vibrant characters' stories moved into other genres: *George Shrinks* appeared daily on PBS, *Rolie Polie Olie* turned into a television series from Disney, and *A Day with Wilbur Robinson* became the animated feature film *Meet the Robinsons*. The beauty of the illustrations, done mostly in oil or acrylic, coupled with narratives tinged with mythic themes and characters but tempered by humor, appealed not only to children but also to adults.

Joyce's work in animation came with an invitation from John Lasseter to work on Disney/Pixar's *Toy Story*, the first feature film to be made entirely with computer-generated imagery. (It was released by Walt Disney Pictures in 1995.) Joyce went on to create conceptual characters for *A Bug's Life* (1998) and art design for many other films from DreamWorks, Twentieth Century Fox, and Disney, including *Meet the Robinsons* and *Mr. Magorium's Wonder Emporium* (about a marvelous toy store owned by an eccentric 243-year-old). During these years, he managed to decorate the Christmas windows of Saks Fifth Avenue and create covers for the *New Yorker* as well.

Enter Brandon Oldenburg, a Texan who, after graduating from the prestigious Ringling College of Art and Design, cofounded Reel FX Creative Design Studios in Dallas. Just as Joyce grew up drawing, Oldenburg grew up making movies. A longtime fan, in 1998 he approached Joyce about a possible collaboration. The partnership has never ended. According to Trish Farnsworth-Smith, managing director at howdy ink, a private company Joyce ran from his studio at Centenary College, Oldenburg says that they "get each other on so many levels" (personal interview).

A few years later, Lampton Enochs left Katrina-ravaged New Orleans with his business partner, Alissa Kantrow, to found what became Louisiana Production Consultants, a business designed to bring movie and television projects to North Louisiana. After a meeting of the partners with Joyce and his wife, Elizabeth, the four became friends and had the idea of founding a studio in Shreveport. With Enochs to cover the financial and contractual aspects of the venture and Joyce working his magic, adding Brandon Oldenburg to the team was the next step. Despite his ongoing collaboration with Joyce, Oldenburg, living happily in Dallas with his wife and two young children, was not eager to move. An additional impediment was that he had been hired as creative director for the upcoming London tour of Michael Jackson, his longtime favorite musician. Jackson's sudden death changed Oldenburg's future. He put his Dallas home on the market the next weekend and prepared to move to Shreveport. And so in August 2009, Enochs, Oldenburg, and Joyce founded the animation and visual effects studio called Moonbot. Trish Farnsworth-Smith, who had first worked with Joyce on projects with the Shreveport Regional Arts Council, came on board to help with managing howdy ink and then became head of production at Moonbot Studios, which means she keeps everything running the way it is supposed to run.

The new collaborations required new work space. The Centenary College studio was not adequate to house the rapidly growing Moonbot Studios. Even after acquiring larger quarters, however, Joyce opted to maintain offices at the college, where as artist in residence he gives workshops from time to time. He also accepts interns from Centenary, who get firsthand experience working with animation and film.

The staff grew as well. Instead of two and a half people, there were eventually over seventy Bots, many of them graduates of the Ringling School of Design or from the School of Design at the North Carolina School of the Arts. The technology people often came from Texas A&M. They were mostly from the South, and all of them were bright and creative. The team was close, often socializing at a pool party or watching movies together at the studio.

Where do the story ideas come from? Joyce claims much of his work is autobiographical. The Rolie Polies, for example, are caricatures of members of his family, which he calls "a congenial horde of southern screwballs" (personal interview). Almost everything in *A Day with Wilbur Robinson* has some basis in truth, he says, even the singing frogs. As a boy, Joyce raised frogs from tadpoles, and in the summer they were everywhere. Since listening to Louis Armstrong records was a popular family activity, Joyce combined the two experiences in *Wilbur Robinson* by creating animated frogs that sing like Louis Armstrong. Sometimes the genesis of a story element is less literal. He claims that writing is his way of dealing with both the good and the painful things in his life. In elementary school, he says, he coped with math anxiety by making stories and drawings in which "the vengeful number 5s" did battle with a child who had a giant eraser cannon that would eradicate them.

The truth is that Joyce's ideas can come from anything—an old movie, a song, a random observation. *George Shrinks,* for example, is based on *King Kong*—in reverse. Where King Kong was too big for everything, George spends his time in a world in which he is too small. Whatever their source, the stories are marked by an absence of adult cynicism and the presence of an ability to stimulate the imagination. As Joyce said in an online chat at CNN.com: "I try to make television that actually stimulates that animation gland and drives [young viewers] almost into an imaginative conniption fit. I want them so jazzed after watching one of my shows that they can hardly stand it, that they have to go out and tell somebody or do something or reenact what they have seen by using imaginative play."

Part of the attraction of Joyce's works is that beneath the fantasy and whimsy lie important themes. Repeatedly, the reader/viewer is confronted with the importance of responsibility, love, friendship, kindness, and curiosity. The characters demonstrate the value of believing in possibilities, experiencing the power of daydreams, and practicing basic, everyday goodness. A comment made in *E. Aster Bunnymund and the Warrior Eggs at the Earth's Core!* makes it clear that at the top of the pyramid of good things is the imagination. Speaking of the magical book written by Katherine, one of the major characters, the narrator says: "The ink and paper she used were ordinary, but her mind, her imagination, was what gave the words and pictures their great power: the power to connect her to anyone who read her stories" (34). The observation seems to identify the source of the extraordinary pull of Joyce's own works as well.

As Moonbot Studios grew, the imagination began working overtime, producing an abundance of projects. Chief among them was the "Guardians of Childhood" series, which was designed to appear in picture book, chapter book, and film form. The four novels and three picture books that have come out so far were published by Simon & Schuster, and Joyce was executive producer for the animated feature film based on his series at DreamWorks Animation. They tell, each in its own way, the backstories of some of childhood's favorite characters, such as the Tooth Fairy, the Easter Bunny, and the Sand Man. That is, they focus on who the famous characters were and what they did before they became icons. Readers will be surprised to find, for example, that Saint Nick was once a headstrong young warrior who used his skill with weaponry to plunder treasuries around the world. The stories have heroes and villains, and the forces of good and evil do battle, creating a powerful mythic quality. They reflect Joyce's comment made in a speech to the annual meeting of the American Library Association in 2011. "Kids," he said, "need to believe in wonder and heroes and good things."

Other recent projects at Moonbot include writing, producing, and designing an adaptation of the picture book *The Leaf Men and the Brave Good Bugs* as a computer-animated feature film released by Blue Sky Studios in 2013 under the title *Leaf Men*. Another recent work, making its appearance in 2014, is *The Numberlys*, a short film and a book that retell the 1927 silent classic *Metropolis* for children. The Numberlys are beings who, lacking an alphabet, use numbers instead of letters. With an app for interactive viewing, the viewer can break the numbers apart to make new shapes in a series of games.

William Joyce and Moonbot Studios received increased public attention when *The Fantastic Flying Books of Mr. Morris Lessmore*, Moonbot's first project, won the 2012 Academy Award for Best Animated Short Film. It also won six major awards in addition to the Oscar. The city of Shreveport, having long embraced Moonbot Studios, celebrated the wins with a ticker-tape parade and the mayor's declaration of a public holiday in its honor. Surprisingly, *Morris Lessmore* started out as an idea for a book, but as the working relationship with Brandon Oldenburg prospered and Moonbot Studios came into being, it turned into a film. Lampton Enochs was a coproducer.

Morris Lessmore is notable for its use of miniatures, computer animation, 2D animation, matte paintings, and even practical shots of dust and debris, but it became cutting edge when Ken and Keith Hanson of Twin Engine Labs headed up a team that created an app for it that made "interactive storytelling" possible. (Apple brought out the iPad when the film was in the middle of production.) The reader/viewer actually becomes part of Morris Lessmore's world through games, hidden content, even an opportunity to play the piano, inviting children to puzzle out the secrets and to be curious. Not surprisingly, in the first week after its release, it moved to the top of Apple's iPad app chart in the United States, and at different times it has been the top book app in twenty-one countries. In addition to highly positive reviews and many awards, it also won App of the Year for 2011 from *Apps Magazine* and Best iPad app at *iPad Insight* blog. The multimedia project *Morris Lessmore* stands as an example of the wide range of creativity William Joyce and his colleagues have to tell stories in new ways and using new media. What began as an idea for a book became an animated short film that generated an app. The printed book was released in June 2012.

Despite the extensive use of technology to produce *Morris Lessmore*, the film actually celebrates the joys of reading. It tells the story of a book lover who cares for a living library, then writes a book that recounts "his joys and sorrows, of all that he knew and everything that he hoped." As the lush visual images roll by, the soundtrack plays "Pop Goes the Weasel," sometimes joyously, sometimes mournfully. The whole reflects Joyce's response to seeing how stories gave solace to children displaced by Hurricane Katrina, an experience that reinforced his belief in the power of books to heal troubled souls. The children were physically in crowded shelters, but their imaginations took them to a better place.

The magic of *Morris Lessmore*, and of William Joyce's works in general, lies not only in the stories themselves but in the visual narratives as well. Studying great illustrators such as Maxfield Parrish, Beatrix Potter, and N. C. Wyeth, Joyce developed a sophisticated technique that uses a variety of media, including watercolor, oil, acrylic, pen and ink, colored pencils, and computer graphics. The result is illustrations that are hauntingly beautiful but which at the same time have the power to surprise and delight. The more one looks at them, the more one sees. Faces and hats and animals appear in what initially may look to be only a cloud. While his illustrations are highly collectible, they are not for sale these days. Although he sold some early in his career, today Joyce keeps the originals, many of which hung on the walls of Moonbot Studios.

Despite the studio's many successes, work slowed after the untimely deaths of Joyce's wife and daughter from terminal illnesses. To deal with financial problems, the management team explored alternatives that would have taken Moonbot away from Shreveport. After a year or so, however, Joyce decided to rebuild. "Shreveport is my hometown," he said. "The idea of home and family is a part of all my work. So keeping Moonbot here makes every kind of sense" (www.williamjoyce.com/). New collaborations with television and feature companies promise to renew the studio's creative output.

William Joyce's honors have been almost as numerous as the books, films, and apps. As the new century began, *Newsweek* magazine named him one of the one hundred people to watch in the new millennium. Then came the three Emmys for the *Rolie Polie Olie* series that aired on the Disney Channel, and in 2008 Joyce received the Louisiana Writer of the Year Award for his contribution to the "literary intellectual heritage of Louisiana." But it is not the awards that keep Joyce writing and drawing. Instead, he seems driven by his own imagination to create books, films, television, and art that speak to the imagination of others. In many ways he is like Katherine in *E. Aster Bunnymund:* "She would sometimes write stories that were different from what had happened but were about how she felt or what she wished had been . . . she needed to do it" (244–45). It seems William Joyce needs to do it as well.

WORKS BY WILLIAM JOYCE

BOOKS

(all books are both written and illustrated by William Joyce, except as noted)

My First Book of Nursery Tales, written by Marianna Mayer (1983)
Tammy and the Gigantic Fish, written by Bethany Roberts (1984)
William Joyce's Mother Goose (1984)
George Shrinks (1985)
Shoes, written by Elizabeth Winthrop (1986)
Dinosaur Bob and His Adventures with the Family Lazardo (1988)
Robots (1988)
Humphrey's Bear, written by Jan Wahl (1989)
A Day with Wilbur Robinson (1990)
Some of the Adventures of Rhode Island Red, written by Stephen Manes (1990)
Nicholas Cricket, written by Joyce Maxner (1991)
Bently & Egg (1992)
Don't Wake the Princess: Hopes, Dreams, and Wishes, cover art (1993)
Santa Calls (1993)
A Wiggly, Jiggly, Joggly Tooth, written by Bill Hawley (1995)
The Leaf Men and the Brave Good Bugs (1996)
Buddy (1997)
Life with Bob, board book (1998)
Baseball Bob, board book (1999)
The Art of Robots (2004)
The Art of Rise of the Guardians (2012)
The Fantastic Flying Books of Mr. Morris Lessmore (2012)
The Mischievians (2013)
A Bean, a Stalk and a Boy Named Jack (2014)
The Numberlys, co-illustrated with Christina Ellis (2014)
Billy's Booger (2015)

Rolie Polie Olie series

Rolie Polie Olie (1999)
Rolie Polie Olie: How Many Howdys? board book (1999)

Rolie Polie Olie: Little Spot of Color, board book (2000)
Rolie Polie Olie: Polka Dot! Polka Dot! board book (2000)
Snowie Rolie (2000)
Rolie Polie Olie Character Books: Olie, Spot, Zowie, Billie (2001)
Big Time Olie (2002)
Busy Books (2002)
Sleepy Time Olie (2002)
Peekaboo, You! board book (2002)
Rolie Polie Shapes, board book (2002)
Be My Pal! board book (2002)
Rocket Up, Rolie! (2002)

The Guardians of Childhood Series

The Man in the Moon (2011)
Nicholas St. North and the Battle of the Nightmare King, with Laura Geringer (2011)
E. Aster Bunnymund and the Warrior Eggs at the Earth's Core! (2012)
The Sandman: The Story of Sanderson Mansnoozie (2012)
Toothiana: Queen of the Tooth Fairy Armies (2012)
The Sandman and the War of Dreams (2013)
Jack Frost (2015)

FILMS

Toy Story, concept artwork (1995)
Buddy, screenwriter (1997)
A Bug's Life, concept artwork (1998)
Rolie Polie Olie, creator (1998–2004)
George Shrinks, creator (2000–2001)
Robots, writer, producer, and production designer (2005)
Meet the Robinsons, writer and executive producer (2007)
Mr. Magorium's Wonder Emporium, production designer (2007)
The Fantastic Flying Books of Mr. Morris Lessmore, codirector with Brandon Oldenburg (2011)
Rise of the Guardians, writer and executive producer (2012)

Epic, writer, production designer, and executive producer (2013)
The Leaf Men, writer, producer, and designer (2013)
The Numberlys, director and writer (2013)
The Scarecrow, executive producer (2013)
The Cask of Amontillado, director (2014)
Silent, executive producer (2014)

WORKS CITED

Joyce, William. Annual Meeting of American Library Association, New Orleans, June 25, 2011.

———. Online chat, September 29, 2000. CNN Interactive, www.cnn.com/chat/transcripts/2000/9/29/joyce/index.html.

———. *E. Aster Bunnymund and the Warrior Eggs at the Earth's Core!* New York: Atheneum Books for Young Readers, 2012.

———. *The Fantastic Flying Books of Mr. Morris Lessmore*. Film. Directed by William Joyce and Brandon Oldenburg. Shreveport: Moonbot Studios, 2011.

———. Personal interview with Trish Farnsworth-Smith, May 5, 2012.

———. *The World of William Joyce Scrapbook*. New York: HarperCollins, 1997.

"William Joyce." *Encyclopedia of World Biography* online, www.notablebiographies.com/newsmakers2/2006-Ei-La/Joyce-William.html.

http://www.williamjoyce.com/

Julie Kane

Formalist, Confessional Poet, and Playful Stylist

Julie Kane recalls hearing the poet Anne Sexton warn her students against getting carried away by having their name under a poem. "Poetry," she said, "is like a river flowing through you. It is a force that is beyond the individual." The comment resonated with Kane, who recognized from the time she was very young that writing poetry was for her "an instinct, a need" (telephone interview). It proved to be so powerful that poetry became the governing force of her adult life.

The commitment to writing poetry earned Kane early recognition. Her first publication was a poem that ran in the Sunday comics section of a Boston newspaper when she was seven years old. More significantly, she won first prize in the *Mademoiselle* magazine college poetry competition while still an undergraduate at Cornell University. It was the first of many prizes to come. In 2002, for example, she was named the winner of the prestigious National Poetry Series. One of the biggest of all accolades came her way when Governor Bobby Jindal appointed her poet laureate of Louisiana. In that role she gave readings of her poems, worked to broaden the audience for poetry, and helped to promote other Louisiana writers. It was a busy couple of years.

The New Orleans Years

Unlike most of the state's poets laureate, Kane is not native to Louisiana. She was, in fact, born in Boston and educated in the Northeast.

She was a student in the prestigious creative writing program at Cornell University and later was a graduate student at Boston University, where she studied under Anne Sexton. After a year serving as the first woman to hold the George Bennett Fellowship in Writing at Phillips Exeter Academy in New Hampshire, she moved to Baton Rouge, Louisiana, with her husband, who had decided to return to his native state to attend law school at Louisiana State University in 1976. When the marriage broke up, Kane intended to return to the Northeast but on a whim decided to visit New Orleans for a holiday. Like many who go to the city to visit and find themselves wanting to stay long past Jazz Fest or Mardi Gras, Kane decided to stay. The unique architecture, the majestic live oaks, the tropical palm trees, the blues, Café du Monde, the people—all were seductive. Seeing an ad in the *New Orleans Times-Picayune* announcing an opening for a technical editor at a nuclear plant, she decided it was time to leave her position with the East Baton Rouge Parish antipoverty agency, where she had worked initially as a grants writer and later as director of the Planning and Evaluations Department. She applied for the editing job, was hired as a technical writer, and in 1978 moved to New Orleans. The redheaded girl from an Irish family in Boston had found a new home in a culture and ambience that would nourish her dream of being a poet.

Kane was quick to find people of like mind, many of them at the Maple Leaf Bar, a popular New Orleans spot where writers and musicians gather to talk and give readings and play music together. The music has been going on seven nights a week since 1974, and the readings have featured poets such as Maxine Cassin, Everette Maddox, and Yusef Komunyakaa. The Maple Leaf has been featured in stories by Ellen Gilchrist and in numerous poems, some of them by Julie Kane. Three anthologies of poets who have read their work at the Maple Leaf have been published. Kane found there a mutually supportive community of creative personalities bonded by friendship and their love of making art. As she explains it, "We were catching each others' updraft" (telephone interview). Although there was a downside too (too much alcohol, too many damaged lives), her time spent there was a productive period when she worked at developing her craft in the company of colorful companions.

When Kane realized that to have a career in academia she would need a PhD, she enrolled in the doctoral literature program at Louisiana State University but stayed in her adopted city of New Orleans. (During her studies at LSU, she also picked up a minor in creative writing.) As the time approached for writing the dissertation, she moved to St. Gabriel, Louisiana, where she would have the solitude she needed to carry out a scholarly study of the villanelle, a complex poetic form characterized by frequent rhymes and repetition. The move would allow her to hold a teaching assistantship at LSU as well. Her study of the villanelle earned her the Lewis P. Simpson Distinguished Dissertation Award. During her time at LSU she was also given the Academy of American Poets Prize. She remembers this period as a transition from the busyness of New Orleans to the simpler life she would have four years later in Natchitoches, where she was hired to be a visiting poet at Northwestern State University of Louisiana. Like her earlier visit to New Orleans, the move to Natchitoches became permanent, where she was professor in the Language and Communication Department until her retirement in July 2016. Natchitoches, she says, may be smaller and quieter than New Orleans, but compared to St. Gabriel, it fairly bustles. Then, too, it reminds her of New Orleans with its old French influence, its architecture, its river, and its literary history. It even has a "funky little blues club."

The Academic Life

A few years after joining the Northwestern faculty, Kane was chosen to be a Fulbright lecturer in creative writing and American studies at Vilnius Pedagogical University in Lithuania. The adventure led to several interesting developments in her writing life. In the past, she had had the experience of translating into English a sequence of poems

Victor Hugo wrote after his daughter drowned. (There is a strong possibility of their being published one day as a chapbook.) When she began to exchange poems and letters with a Lithuanian poet and friend, she realized how few of that culture's poems were available to readers from other countries and took steps to get some of them into print in English. Protesting that her Lithuanian is mostly tourist speech, today she works with a native speaker who provides rough translations from that language for her to polish into poems.

A serious brush with cancer in 2002 made Kane increasingly reflective about her life. She found it disturbing that although she had made sacrifices for her poetry, sometimes forgoing socially valued experiences that would have interfered with her writing, she had not significantly connected with the public. She had earned her PhD and published two books, but she had yet to gain a substantial following of readers. In an effort to leave a lasting mark on the world, she polished up a manuscript of her poems and sent it out to several contests. The affirmation she needed reached her in Lithuania when she received notice that she was a finalist in the National Poetry Series, judged by Maxine Kumin. Being named the winner led to the publication of *Rhythm and Booze* in 2003, giving her a book with national distribution. It confirmed that she was a poet with a future. Commenting on the importance of poetry prizes, Kane points to the significance of this one for her career not only because it provided reassurance that the work was good or that it introduced new readers to her poems but because being affirmed by someone whom she respected was deeply gratifying.

Kane's other books of poetry are *Body and Soul* and *Jazz Funeral*, which was the winner of the Donald Justice Poetry Prize. A memoir cowritten with Kiem Do, *Counterpart: A South Vietnamese Naval Officer's War*, recounts the war experiences of a high-ranking officer in the Vietnamese navy and, more generally, examines the cultural changes that the war brought to Vietnam. Her latest is *Paper Bullets*, which R. S. Gwynn described in a blurb on the back cover as "a bag of tricks ranging from couplets to limericks to triolets, with enough left over to feed the multitudes who have long been starved for a book of poetry that combines humor with wisdom, acid wit with a spoonful of sugar, and such a large portion of good will towards all that it makes me want to celebrate."

The Poems

Julie Kane has been described as a formalist, a confessional poet, a playful stylist. Somehow she is all these things and more. The formalism, which has seemed to grow with the years, is so subtle that the reader hardly notices the frequent rhyming, the sly repetitions, the smooth iambic meters. Asked why she is given to using complex poetic forms, she answers that formal constraints drive her in surprising directions. They make her do what she did not know she would do; they make her "go deeper." She also likes the music that meter and rhyme create. She calls it "poetry for the ear" (telephone interview).

The villanelle, which she seems to write with uncanny ease, is a case in point. Even its definition is hard to follow. Try this: it is a nineteen-line poem that has only two rhymes and repeats two of the lines according to a set pattern. Line 1 is repeated as lines 6, 12, and 18; line 3 as lines 9, 15, and 19. The first and third lines recur as a rhymed couplet at the end in a stanza of four lines. And that is just the bare outline. Like many complicated items, the villanelle is more easily explained by citing an example. Take, for instance, Kane's "Villanelle for Joe, on My Birthday," in which she characteristically bends the rules a bit by varying the refrain lines. She describes the liberties as being analogous to a jazz musician improvising on a recognizable melody.

> For once you're going to be like other guys,
> not call me even though you said you'd call
> to wish me happy birthday. My "surprise"

will be a silent phone and bloodshot eyes,
a soggy Kleenex wadded in a ball,
because you're going to be like other guys.

Beginning in July of eighty-five
for all these years your reedy Southern drawl
has wished me happy birthday—no surprise,

a sort of Northern Star to plot course by
through middle age, its map of losses, all
that makes us, once unique, like other guys.

An old pop record—*Judy's Turn to Cry?*—
that you, my fellow boomer, would recall,
expressed it: *What a birthday surprise!*

You'll stand me up and won't apologize
this year, old friend, but only by default.
You had to die to be like other guys,
your constant heart, time's loveliest surprise.
(*Rhythm and Booze* 51)

The villanelle was initially a form used by French poets; it did not appear in English until the second half of the nineteenth century, when it became the genre of fairly lighthearted poems. Kane explains that her attraction to it lies in a correspondence between the way it breaks its repeated patterns in the last stanza and her own intention to move away from alcohol, which had been part of a family pattern and for a while her own. As she says, "You can't tell a story or make an argument in a villanelle, but you can deal with subject matter that goes around repeatedly" (telephone interview).

Even when discussing the craft of writing poetry, Kane sounds poetic. For example, she compares working with a new form to what happens when a cook makes French toast. She points out that the first slice is likely to be splotchy and rough, but the second and third will be smooth and golden. And so it is with poems. The first poem in a new form may turn out to be awkward and "clunky," but with practice its patterns are internalized, and the process comes to seem natural and comfortable.

As for being a confessional poet, she certainly was subject to the right influences for becoming one. Having studied briefly with Anne Sexton (who committed suicide only a few weeks after Kane enrolled in her class) and having lionized Sylvia Plath (the poet, novelist, and short story writer who also took her own life), she could have adopted their poetic practice without surprising anyone. Kane recognizes their influence in her work but prefers to call herself a "neo-confessional poet." Her own personal experience is the basis of many of her poems, but in the end there is not total correspondence between a real event or encounter and the poem itself. Life's incidents are just the beginning of the poem, not the fully realized work.

In addition to being a formalist and a self-described neo-confessional poet, Kane frequently assumes a playful, even mischievous voice in her works. Readers often comment that her poems sound conversational, partly the result of using words that rarely show up in poems—words such as *bugs, amputated, primordial ooze.* Kane rejects the idea that was common in ancient Greece or the sixteenth century that certain language is poetic. Instead, the poetic element for her resides in the shimmering quality that certain experiences have, a resonance they have about them. The poetic is not so much connected to language as it is to images and encounters. In short, unlike much contemporary poetry, her poems invite the reader in. They are accessible, though never frivolous in thought or in craft. Consider the opening stanzas of "The Bartender Quits Drinking":

> The Mater Dolorosa parking lot
> is always full on Fridays during Lent.
> I hear them chanting Stations of the Cross

as I double-park for the pastry shop,
this boozeless season giving us a bent
for doughnuts, candy, soda pop.
(*Rhythm and Booze* 16)

The source of the playful persona she often assumes, she says, is Irish humor. As an example, she remembers her father's reaction to clumsy medical attendants who couldn't seem to get him moved from his hospital room to a treatment center when he was having a second heart attack. They got the wheels of the gurney stuck in the elevator door and, instead of giving him oxygen, managed to pour water down his nose. He laughed, thinking he was going to die before the incompetent attendants could get him the help he needed. Irish humor indeed.

Kane's concern for making "poetry for the ear" took a literal turn when she began to collaborate with composers to turn her poems into musical pieces. Her early work with Libby Larsen, she says, was the result of sheer luck. When Larsen came across Kane's newly published "Reasons for Loving the Harmonica" in an anthology of poems about music, she got in touch with Kane asking to use it for a piece she would later write for the American Boychoir in Princeton, New Jersey. It was premiered by that group at the Sixtieth Anniversary Gala Concert in Princeton in 1998 and later performed on tour. Larsen also set the poem "Blond Men" to music; it was premiered at the Ravinia Festival in Chicago. One collaboration has stayed in the family. Kane's niece Dale Trumbore is a composer who has made music with several of her poems, including "The Mermaid Story," "Prayer to Chaos," and "House Made Out of Mud."

In retrospect, it seems that Julie Kane has always known that poetry was a force, like Anne Sexton's "river." She remembers in the elementary grades bringing her English book home on the first day of school and reading all the poems in it that night. She recalls as a child finding blank pages at the end of her favorite book, Hans Christian Andersen's *Fairy Tales*, and knowing that they had been placed there for her to fill up. She was certain that she was meant to write her own fairy tale on them, and she did, spinning a story about a young maiden who has a fairy godmother. Now, many years later, the same conviction that she was meant to write and the belief that writing gives meaning to life sends Kane throughout Louisiana and beyond to read her poems, give workshops, and talk about poetry. She is still filling up the empty pages.

PUBLISHED WORKS BY JULIE KANE

POETRY

"Learning Curve (What They Taught Me)" (n.d.)
"Sex Appeal of the Presidents" (n.d.)
Rosetta (1975)
Two into One, with Ruth Adatia (1982)
Body and Soul (1987)
The Bartender Poems (1991)
Rhythm and Booze (2003)
Alan Doll Rap (2005)
Jazz Funeral (2009)
Paper Bullets (2014)

MEMOIR

Counterpart: A South Vietnamese Naval Officer's War, with Kiem Do (1998)

ANTHOLOGIES

"Thirteen," in *I Wouldn't Thank You for a Valentine: Poems for Young Feminists*, edited by Carol Ann Duffy (1997)

WORKS CITED

Do, Kiem, and Julie Kane. *Counterpart: A South Vietnamese Naval Officer's War.* Annapolis, Md.: Naval Institute Press, 1998.

Kane, Julie. "The Bartender Quits Drinking." *Rhythm and Booze.* Chicago: University of Illinois Press, 2003.

———. Telephone interview, June 21, 2012.

———. "Villanelle for Joe, on My Birthday." *Rhythm and Booze.* Chicago: University of Illinois Press, 2003.

Tom Piazza

A Serious Writer and More

Tom Piazza is a man of many parts, with interests that at first glance may seem unrelated, even incongruous. He is a writer of fiction, nonfiction, and television drama as well as an award-winning commentator on music—jazz, country, and blues. He is also a keen observer of American life, examining it through the lens of popular culture: music, literature, and current events. In that role he has become a vocal advocate for New Orleans, calling it "a small model of all the best of America" (*Devil Sent the Rain* pt. 2, chap. 5). His ability to integrate such disparate pursuits into a meaningful whole speaks to readers, viewers, and music lovers alike.

Even the characters and settings of Piazza's fiction are diverse. Drawn from a wide variety of people and places, they reflect distinctly different cultural backgrounds. For example, his *Blues and Trouble*, a collection of twelve stories set in cities and towns across America, moves from Brownsville, Texas, to New York City to Memphis, Tennessee, and features widely differing characters that range from a coarse-speaking bar performer to a down-on-his-luck drifter to a pair of furniture deliverymen given to outrageous behavior. They are drawn from all social and economic classes, races, and backgrounds. Uniting the diverse stories is their disturbing picture of a troubled America, one characterized by cultural uncertainties, personal loneliness, and moral ambiguity. Their characters are unrooted. They are searching for personal identity, for a sense of belonging.

Piazza's novels pursue similar themes. *My Cold War* criticizes the superficiality of American culture through the character of John Delano, a history professor who lectures on the "surfaces" of the past. Brushing away deeper observations, he says: "Only the surfaces of history are real. The understructure is what is provisional and gets blown away with the wind" (39). Piazza's more recent novel *A Free State* is a radical departure in subject, going back to 1855 to tell the story of an escaped slave who hides in plain sight as a minstrel in a blackface show in Philadelphia while he is pursued by a brutal slave chaser. The time and characters may have changed, but again the question of identity arises: who is this man who is struggling to be free? And what is the difference between what you see and what is?

In contrast to the ambiguity and complexity of his narratives, Piazza creates images that are sharp and precise. He has an extraordinary eye for detail that creates the look and feel of the fictional settings with power and authenticity. Take, for example, this passage from *My Cold War:*

> The living room was filled with furry and nubbed over-stuffed velvet and brocade furniture from the 1920s, lamps with fringed shades, but we spent most of our time in the finished basement, a low-ceilinged room lined with varnished pine wainscoting and furnished with rattan chairs. My grandmother would lay out pieces of Swiss cheese on waxed paper on the table under the fluorescent-ring ceiling lamp. Upstairs was a sunny, old-fashioned tiled kitchen and the living room, and then, up a long flight of carpeted stairs, the bedroom level, where my deaf aunt had painted a swan on the pink tiles over the toilet. Through a door narrow enough to belong to a broom closet, a steep set of wooden stairs led up to a finished attic, which had been my father's room, where old books and photos were to be found everywhere in the four dormers. After dinner I would sneak away from the table to go up there and look over at the houses and trees and see the light in the

> clock tower at the top of Biener Pontiac winking against the sunset like the evening star. (39)

Sometimes metaphor replaces literal description, especially when a character's emotional or mental state is under examination. In "A Servant of Culture," one of the stories in *Blues and Trouble,* Piazza writes: "He feels waves of anger speeding along his nerves, like urgent messages over phone lines. He imagines that anyone could see the anger, coming off his face like heat waves off of a car hood at the beach" (60). And in *My Cold War* the narrator says, "I tested the idea, the way you might test the ice on a pond with your foot, tentatively, to see how much weight it could take" (135). In the same novel the city's air becomes a force of nature: "Outside the afternoon flowed heavy, hot, and golden through the Dallas streets; the late sunlight clanged off the sides of buildings and filled the air, viscous and radioactive, like some kind of atomic beer syrup through the open door, it leaked into the cavernous bar where we were sitting and spilled across the maroon-painted floor" (66).

Sometimes the language becomes lyrical, taking on the qualities of music. In "Losing Hand," another of the stories in *Blues and Trouble,* the reader finds sentences such as: "I'm going to wait until the last moment to leave, until the sun comes up like a gangster over Mulholland Drive and the gypsy women have gone to sleep and I can see the writing on the wall. As I drive to the airport through the cool, shadowed streets, I will fade in her mind like a constellation in the morning sky. She'll wait until the plane takes off and the gauzy clouds waft past the windows like static gathering as a radio station fades, and then she'll emerge like a fugitive into the brilliant sunlight and run to the ocean to make a new start" (163).

Music is often referenced by Piazza and by those who read him. It is always present in his fiction. *Blues and Trouble,* for example, is said to be arranged in imitation of a twelve-bar blues, and some critics have noted that the stories are held together by an overall structure that is musical—that the first eleven compose a blues suite, and the last story, "Charley Patton," which consists of twelve paragraphs, serves as a coda to the piece as a whole. *My Cold War*, which is not directly about music at all, has many references to music, including a multipage digression about a gathering of musicians at Narragansett Bay, Rhode Island. In the television drama *Treme*, for which Piazza has been a principal writer, music does not simply furnish background. It becomes a character.

The frequency of references to music is not surprising, considering the fact that Piazza was interested and involved in it early on. At sixteen he became the youngest writer to appear in *DownBeat*, and while an undergraduate at Williams College, he organized a jazz festival and did a weekly radio show called "Home for the Bewildered." After college he moved to New York, where he hoped to become a composer and jazz pianist. While working a variety of jobs there, he studied piano, wrote music for a West Side theater workshop, and played jazz piano in bars and nightclubs. As Piazza described his attitude at the time, "Jazz music was alive in every line—it depended for its rationale on being alive in every line, the sense of bets being entered, and antes increased, as the soloist's thought was spun out" (*Devil Sent the Rain* pt. 2, chap. 11). At the same time, he began publishing articles about music in the *Village Voice*, *Newsday*, and *DownBeat* and worked as a messenger at the *New Yorker*. (He even sold a story about jazz to the magazine, but it was never published.)

In time, his music articles and commentaries garnered increasing interest, eventually making him a three-time winner of the ASCAP Deems Taylor Award for Music Writing for his books *The Guide to Classic Recorded Jazz* and *Understanding Jazz* and for his Oxford American CD set, *Martin Scorsese Presents the Blues: A Musical Journey*. Other pieces have been anthologized in publications such as *Best Music Writing 2000*, *The Oxford American Book of Great Music Writing*, and *Studio A: The Bob Dylan Reader*. It should be noted that his writings about music are not just histories or promotional pieces. He seeks, as in *Understanding Jazz*, to help listeners reach a deeper appreciation of the indigenous art forms he loves.

He helps people discover how to listen by noticing form, style, and instrumentation.

Piazza profiles individual musicians in part 1 of *Devil Sent the Rain: Music and Writing in Desperate America,* people like Bob Dylan, Charley Patton, and Jimmie Rodgers, who attract his interest because he sees them as "American originals" (chap. 12). In the introduction he notes that the essays in the opening section of the book represent "a kind of optimism about the basic template of American possibility." After Hurricane Katrina in 2005 and the government mismanagement that followed, however, optimism was harder to sustain. Part 2 of *Devil Sent the Rain* is composed of pieces that deal with those events, along with commentaries on several other subjects of interest to him, such as Norman Mailer, who, Piazza says, made him want to be a writer. Part 3 he calls "a coda . . . a kind of post-post Katrina stocktaking—and a very short column, written before the storm, about things that endure" (intro.). In fact, the book overall, according to Piazza, was a stocktaking, a matter of going over things that were important to him and to the country as a whole.

Katrina was not only a disaster for New Orleans; it became a turning point for Tom Piazza's relationship with the public. As the extent of the tragedy unfolded, Piazza, appalled not only by his own losses but also by the city's physical destruction, the government ineptitude, the uprooted lives, and human suffering, began to write. In the five weeks that followed, he produced *Why New Orleans Matters,* a manifesto that made him an unofficial spokesman for the city's recovery. Its defense of the city's life and culture and its celebration of the community's diversity, mixed with Piazza's anger and mourning, became a powerful appeal for rebuilding. It also made Piazza a household name and led to speaking engagements and interviews throughout the country.

At first glance, Piazza would seem to have been an unlikely defender of New Orleans. He was a native of Long Island, educated in New England, and lived for a time in New York City. When he made it to Jazz Fest in 1987, however, he knew that he had found where he was meant to be. By then he was in his early thirties, writing for Gordon Lish's avant-garde literary magazine the *Quarterly* and some music publications. These endeavors led him to enroll at the prestigious Iowa Writers' Workshop, where he earned an MFA in fiction writing. It was not until 1994, when he went to New Orleans to interview singer-songwriter Dr. John upon publication of his autobiography, *Under a Hoodoo Moon*, that Piazza actually moved to the city.

The move was a significant one for more than professional reasons. It was in his new city that Piazza met and fell in love with prominent New Orleans attorney Mary Howell. For almost two decades they have shared their mutual affection (bordering on passion) for the city, its people, and its music, but in summers they head for Malden, Missouri, where they enjoy a retreat that resembles a holiday from the last century. Although Tom reserves time and space to work in his writing cabin, with no television or radio, Tom, Mary, and their visitors amuse themselves with badminton, croquet, and ringtoss. They hold an annual competition for throwing walnuts into a walnut tree, and one year they held a writers' night in which everyone read from current works. There is a notebook always open for people to make comments and remarks that sometimes result in a collective poem. Music, of course, is always present, and whoever is there is encouraged to perform.

New Orleans, however, is never far from Piazza's mind. After publishing *Why New Orleans Matters*, he returned to it by using fiction to depict the personal and collective disruption caused by Katrina and the broken levees. The title of the novel, *City of Refuge*, was taken from a gospel blues song sung by Blind Willie Johnson, who made records in New Orleans in the 1920s. As Piazza explained to the *New Orleans Times-Picayune*, "Everybody in the book in some kind of way, needs some kind of refuge, either as a result of the storm or before the storm. At some point the characters need to find their way out of and readjust their relationship to a place of—what's the word?—not acceptance, not comfort, not necessarily safety even" (Larson).

City of Refuge pays homage to New Orleans' unique culture, but like its nonfiction predecessor, it does not ignore or excuse the city's negative aspects. It acknowledges the poverty, the corruption, the racism, that exists, but at the same time it asserts that New Orleans is a city that deserves respect from all. As Piazza comments in *Why New Orleans Matters:* "New Orleans is . . . a city of elegance, beauty, and refinement. It is also a city of violence, poor education, and such extreme poverty you'd have to see it to believe it" (pt. 1, chap. 5). Nevertheless, the novel celebrates the city's multiculturalism and the fact that "all social and ethnic and economic levels of society have somehow managed to fashion a distinct and beautiful culture out of the tension among their differences" (Piazza website). The televised drama *Treme* depicts that same vision of the city. Its rich characters and psychological subtlety capture the complex organism that is New Orleans.

City of Refuge is a structurally complicated narrative that follows the lives of two families, one black, one white, during and after Hurricane Katrina. (Some lesser characters bear close resemblance to actual New Orleanians.) For the most part, the two families are presented in separate chapters, since, as Piazza explained in a radio interview, they would not likely have been together in reality. However, they both appear in chapters 5 and 6, in which the hurricane gives them a shared experience, and in the final chapter. Their stories are interwoven with nonfiction passages about the storm, the flooding, and the nation's reaction to it.

Chapter 13 of *City of Refuge* is notable for its scrambled presentation. The chaos of the flooded city with its homeless population is reflected in the jumbled arrangement of the scene, making what the narrator calls "a sequential narrative" impossible. It reads:

> Everything was on overload, and what would be the use of trying to construct a sequential story when, as one day went by, and then another, and another, time itself was perverted, turned into a garbage dump under the hot blue sky. The drawer had been pulled out of every dresser and the contents

> dumped on the floor; every narrative was twisted and mocked, torn out of any context and flung down next to the grandmother of someone else's narrative; elderly people in open-backed hospital gowns, ripped out of their own story and set down with their IVs in wheelchairs in the middle of the street, hungry, deposited by someone who left to save themselves, not even wished good luck, madness dragging at the cuffs of your pants, dragging like devils in the pit, hissing at you, beckoning, the palsy in that old lady's face, the old man with a plaid short-sleeve shirt and a green suitcase.

If the characters in *City of Refuge* are confronted with questions about who they are and how they are to live, the lives of those who appear in other stories and novels set across America are no less discordant. Their days are unsatisfying and incomplete, reflecting Piazza's dark, disturbing vision of America. That vision is epitomized by the narrator's description of Brownsville, Texas, in the story of the same name. He comments: "I picture Brownsville as a place under a merciless sun where one-eyed dogs stand in the middle of dusty, empty streets staring at you and hot breeze blows inside your shirt and there's nowhere to go. It's always noon, and there are no explanations required. I'm going to Brownsville exactly because I've got no reason to go there" (4). This attitude is echoed by the narrator of *My Cold War* as he addresses the state of American culture directly: "It was as if people couldn't identify with an image of America that was anything less than all good. . . . They had been presented with a transcendent vision of the nation's promise and destiny, but without the leavening sense of the undertow of the world's inevitable barbarism" (152–53). The situation is not without hope, however. As Piazza commented in an interview on the *PBS NewsHour:* "I think if there is a promise to American culture, it might reside somewhere in the notion that what's most important is where people go, where people are able to go, given where they started. So there is always this tension between . . . the place of origin and the path that one takes through all this different variety that we encounter in American culture" (Brown).

Such passages have caused critics such as A. L. Kennedy, writing in the *San Francisco Chronicle*, to say that Piazza's genre is "the American novel of ideas." Others have called him "the thinking reader's novelist." It is a judgment with which he would probably not disagree. In an interview with Susan Larson he commented, "I've always felt that the difference between serious fiction and non-serious fiction is that non-serious fiction can lead you to believe that things don't have a cost. If a bill is not presented for the choices a character makes, it's not serious in my view."

Such artistry, purpose, and reflection have not gone unnoticed. Piazza has been the recipient of a long list of awards. A recent tribute came from the Louisiana Center for the Book in the State Library of Louisiana, which honored him in 2015 with the Louisiana Writer Award, given annually to recognize outstanding contributions to Louisiana's literary and intellectual life. Other honors include the Faulkner Society Award for the Novel given to *My Cold War*, the James Michener Award for *Blues and Trouble*, and the Willie Morris Award for Southern Fiction for *City of Refuge*. The Young Leadership Council / Literacy Alliance reading initiative, One Book, One New Orleans, made *City of Refuge* its selection for the year it was published, and the New Orleans Gulf South Booksellers Association and the Louisiana Endowment for the Humanities honored *Why New Orleans Matters* as the book of the year in 2005.

Colleges and universities have honored Piazza in their own way. He has held the Eudora Welty Chair for Southern Studies at Millsaps College and has been the Visiting Writer in Residence at Loyola University, the Trias Visiting Writer at Hobart and William Smith Colleges, a Teaching-Writing Fellow at the University of Iowa, and a core faculty member at the Bennington Writing Seminars. He has delivered lectures and readings at the University of California at Berkeley, the University of North Carolina, the Chautauqua Institution, the National Arts Club, and the Library of Congress.

Tom Piazza may be a man of many interests and passions, but it is clear that he is a serious writer, regardless of the genre or subject. His recognition of the significance of writing and its power to tie all things together in a way no other medium can, so evident in both his fiction and nonfiction, is confirmed by a statement that appears in *Devil Sent the Rain*. In the introduction to those essays, he says: "The written word is not simply a less efficient delivery system for information or opinion. In the private space shared by the writer and the reader, one individual soul encounters another and a spell is cast, created by both of them." Now that's a serious writer.

PUBLISHED WORKS BY TOM PIAZZA

The Guide to Classic Recorded Jazz (1995)
Setting the Tempo: Fifty Years of Great Liner Notes (1996)
Blues and Trouble (1997)
Blues Up and Down (1997)
My Cold War (2004)
Understanding Jazz: Ways to Listen (2005)
Why New Orleans Matters (2005)
City of Refuge (2008)
True Adventures with the King of Bluegrass (2009)
Devil Sent the Rain: Music and Writing in Desperate America (2011)
The Southern Journey of Alan Lomax (2012)
A Free State (2015)

WORKS CITED

Brown, Jeffrey. "Devil Sent the Rain." *PBS NewsHour*, September 16, 2001, www.pbs.org/newshour/art/conversation-tom-piazza-devil-sent-the-rain/.

Kennedy, A. L. "Best Books of 2008." Rev. of *City of Refuge*, by Tom Piazza. *San Francisco Chronicle*, December 21, 2008, M4.

Larson, Susan. "Review of *City of Refuge*, by Tom Piazza." *New Orleans Times-Picayune*, August 17, 2008, n.p.

Piazza, Tom. "Brownsville." *Blues and Trouble*. New York: St. Martin's Press, 1997.

———. *City of Refuge*. HarperCollins e-books, 2008.

———. *Devil Sent the Rain: Music and Writing in Desperate America*. New York Harper, 2011. Kindle edition.

———. "Losing Hand." *Blues and Trouble*. New York: St. Martin's Press, 1997.

———. *My Cold War*. New York: HarperCollins, 2004.

———. "A Servant of Culture." *Blues and Trouble*. New York: St. Martin's Press, 1997.

———. Website. www.tompiazza.com.

———. *Why New Orleans Matters*. New York: HarperCollins, 2005.

Martha Serpas' Balancing Act

If the Roman poet Horace was right in saying that the purpose of literature is "to delight and instruct," then the poems of Martha Serpas clearly fulfill their purpose. They please the reader with lush and vivid imagery; they instruct not by preaching but by provoking thought. Both ends are achieved by the unexpected pairings of words and ideas that are not ordinarily connected and are often outright opposites, contrasting entities that sit on either end of an unmoving seesaw. The result is that her poems could be described as a balancing act.

Serpas herself is a combination of diverse skills and talents. She is, of course, a poet with three books of her own in print. Her first book of poems, *Côte Blanche,* was distinguished by carrying a foreword by Harold Bloom in which he describes Serpas as "in a highly original way, a Catholic devotional poet from Louisiana [who has] perfected this, her first book, across fifteen years." He concludes that "a double handful of these poems may achieve permanence." She has also honored other poets by editing an anthology of Texas and Louisiana poets, and her articles and poems have appeared in such prestigious publications as *Christianity and Literature,* the *New Yorker,* and *Southwest Review.*

To the surprise of some, Serpas was a hospital trauma chaplain for five years before becoming a poet. For two years she worked at Tampa General Hospital in the Clinical Pastoral Education Program, where she trained in trauma response, patient and family care, end-of-life issues, and confidential documentation. From there she moved to

Memorial Hermann Hospital in Houston, Texas, to serve as chaplain. In that capacity she responded on call to crises, trauma, bereavement, and spiritual care situations. In 2012 she returned to Tampa General Hospital to serve as resident chaplain. That period of her life is clearly evident in her poetry, in which the subjects of death and change appear frequently.

Martha Serpas is also a teacher, a role that in her case takes many forms. She is a frequent presenter in classrooms and at conferences, where she discusses issues related to both writing and spirituality. The audiences vary from elementary school students to teachers to inmates of detention homes and members of the American Academy of Religion. She gives readings in bookstores, churches, and schools, and she has served as visiting poet, writer-in-residence, and lecturer at colleges and universities throughout the country, from Yale University to Gustavus Adolphus College in Minnesota. Her more permanent academic positions have included ten years teaching English and writing at the University of Tampa in Florida and her current professorship in the creative writing program at the University of Houston in Texas.

The diversity of Serpas' interests and skills is apparent in the professional societies to which she belongs. She is a member of the American Academy of Religion, the American Association of University Professors, and the Association of Writers and Writing Programs.

Despite her education, her travels, and her professional experiences, Martha Serpas is, inescapably, a product of her birthplace, South Louisiana, the setting that forms the background of much of her poetry. Growing up in Galliano, Serpas early learned Louisiana's natural world, its birds and trees and bayous. Although she moved away from her Gulf Coast homeland after she earned a degree in English at Louisiana State University, she carried those early lessons with her. They accompanied her as she worked toward a master's degree in English at New York University, when she earned her master of divinity degree at Yale Divinity School, and when she completed her doctorate in literature and creative writing at the University of Houston. Those degrees have been put to use in varied ways and diverse settings, but they have not obscured her ties to the Cajun coast. She admits to struggling with writing about Lafourche Parish while composing *Côte Blanche*, her first book of poems, but after Hurricanes Katrina and Rita, she came to the realization that writing about it was a way she could help the people and the place she loves. Although she is by nature a reflective person, she has also become a social advocate for good stewardship of the land. "We have to keep trying to save [the wetlands]," she says, "even though we know it's impossible to save it. It's too late" (Louisiana Book Festival).

The unusual combinations that mark her life are present in her poems as well. Powerfully descriptive, a poem may at first reading seem to offer simple pictures of mundane subjects. "Bully Camp Road," for example, begins with five stanzas cataloging a decaying junkyard. Images never remain just sharp depictions of tangible, physical items in Serpas' poems, however. They are more likely to be suddenly and unexpectedly linked to a seemingly unrelated question or comment. A poem can move quickly from the specific and concrete to the abstract, pulling the reader into participation in exploring a thought in a nonconventional way. The practice can be clearly seen in "Fais Do-Do" (the title referring to a traditional Cajun dance named for the practice of putting children to bed in the dance hall), in which the speaker begins by giving the reader images of the natural beauty of the Gulf Coast in elegant detail. It reads:

> A green heron pulls the sky behind it
> like a zipper. Sharp rows
>
> of clouds fold into themselves, erasing
> the framed blue tide.
>
> Barrier islands disappear into
> the Gulf's gray mouth.

Everywhere something strives to overtake something else:
Grass over a mound of fill dirt, ants over grass,

the rough shading of rust between rows
of sheet metal frustrating the sky.

Boats breast up three deep in every slip,
and, as soon docked, are waved away.

The only music's crickets and lapping,
happy bullfrogs on slick logs.

A rustling skirt of palmettos
around the roots of a modest oak

that appear after hard rain. A fiddle,
or idling motor, moves away.

Then take note of the final three stanzas.

Go to sleep. God will come
in an extended cab for all of us:

the children, the dogs, the poets.
That old Adversary, the Gulf,

our succoring Mother, having given
everything, will carry the whole of us away.
(29–30)

Unusual word pairings often involve the use of liturgical or theological terminology to describe or comment on something not ordinarily linked to religion or belief. It is not too much to say that such use of the language, reflecting her education and her belief, is the norm for Serpas. It has led Harold Bloom to call her "a devotional poet," but her close ties to the physical world and everyday activities set her apart from most writers who carry that label. In "To the Landlady," for example, she juxtaposes observations about laundry and John Deere tractors and a reverential ending. After noting all her landlady's annoying habits, she ends the poem by saying:

> At least you are female, or that word "lord"
> Would come in, confusing with its claims
> Of divinity. You can't *lady* it over me,
>
> Or can you? Lord, Lord, we should own nothing,
> Like You, God, who has given all away.
>
> (52)

Other poems marry even more overt Christian references with common subjects, infusing the latter with a new transcendence. While "Psalm at High Tide," for example, remains rooted in the physical world, it uses explicit religious allusions that turn what is natural or simply ordinary into something that is holy. It reads:

> Rain on the river's vinyl surface:
> water that glitters,
> water that hardly moves,
> its branches witness to trees,
> to fronds, leaves, crab floats, pilings,
> shopping carts, appliances—
> the divine earth takes everything
> in its wounded side
> and gives back wholeness.
> It bears the huddled profane
> and endures the soaking

venerated in its wild swirls—
this river fixed with wooden weirs
radiant in misshapen glory.
(44)

On some occasions Serpas intentionally pays homage to Scripture. The poem "Sand," for instance, echoes Wisdom 11:22. "Poem Found," which takes as its subject the fiasco at the Superdome shelter in the days following Hurricane Katrina, is modeled on the biblical story of creation in Genesis. Its scriptural basis intensifies its biting criticism.

Serpas' penchant for creating unusual combinations extends to the themes that attract her attention. Repeatedly, she addresses the subject of loss but balances it with references to recovery. On other occasions she links destruction with creation, the eternal with the ephemeral, death with rebirth, doubt with faith.

Loss is most evident in her lament over the disappearance of the land and culture she is so closely identified with. In both *Côte Blanche* and *The Dirty Side of the Storm*, she mourns the literal disappearance of the Louisiana wetlands, sometimes because of natural causes, sometimes because of mankind's doing, leading some readers to describe her poems as elegiac. In a poem actually entitled "Eulogy," the speaker comments that she

Can remember the days
before the rigs

Back when you put somebody away
you used to have to dig.
(81–82)

Her criticism of those who would destroy the coast for personal gain is made even more explicit in other poems such as "A Corollary," in which the speaker examines her "misfortune," calling it "this one the steady vanishing / of your birthplace before your eyes" and attributing it to "greed's unbroken refrain" (21). When, in "Tinsel," she notes her community's attempt to save the coastline by using old Christmas trees to stem erosion, Serpas does not celebrate their efforts. Instead, she criticizes them for masking their hypocrisy by donating their trees when their true interest is in "*getting, getting, getting.*"

> On New Year's, we hurl our righteous trees
> on the city truck. Even the treacherous Gulf
> can't wash apostasy off their branches.
> ("Tinsel" 73)

Serpas' concerns about the vanishing land and a vanishing culture have also found expression in her feature-length documentary film, *Veins in the Gulf*. It was the product of an idea her friend Elizabeth Coffman had for them to take a van of film students and poets to the Louisiana coast to document the impact of the loss of wetlands. Through interviews with fishermen, musicians, politicians, and others, the film tells the poignant story of people watching the disappearance of their place, their culture. The filmed images of a crumbling ecosystem and scientists' efforts to slow the process are deeply troubling and disturbing.

On the other hand, Serpas balances an outlook composed of anger and despair over loss of the land, as in the poem "A Future with Hope." She writes, with a subtle allusion to Ecclesiastes:

> Leave hope there where it belongs,
>   on the other side of the levee
> where later it can be found easily,
> its weight, bread crusts on water.
> (83)

Loss of another sort, loss of life itself, is another subject frequently taken up by Serpas. Influenced by her work as a trauma center chaplain, she turns her poetic attention to death and life, body and spirit, change and permanence. She announces her focus with the title of her third collection of poems, *The Diener.* A diener, being the person who runs a morgue, is the link between those paired states of being. (Interestingly, its German root means "servant.") Although loss of the coast to the Gulf remains a major topic, the meeting of the physical and metaphysical takes center stage in this book. The poems retain the rich imagery of her earlier works, but a more enigmatic vision is present. The opening lines of the first poem of the collection, also called "The Diener," indicate the direction the following poems will take, saying,

> We hated the early anatomists
> for showing us how fragile we are,
> how God's image is composite.
>
> (1)

Lives are vulnerable. Life, in the end, is mysterious. Change and stasis are connected. Or, as Serpas writes in "Crossing":

> while they scan
>
> for the new order of things,
> which is the old order renewed, things
>
> moving swiftly but weighed immovable
> in their eyes. Someone might forget
> to declare "good" or "very good" or "evil"

as they drift among their last breaths, their burials,
and this third idle death that frees the soul's
wisdom, still ignorant of its crossing.

Who knows what God will breathe out
after our last breath is drawn?
(27–28)

In the end, one must accept that, as Augustine says in *Confessions* and Serpas ends the book by quoting, "In this world one thing passes away so that another may take its place and the whole be preserved in all its parts" (Augustine, quoted in *Diener* 73).

One cannot close a discussion of Martha Serpas' poems without noting the skill with which she manages her craft. As in other aspects of her writing, she manages to reconcile contrasting entities, in this case traditional practice with innovation. Carefully eschewing conventional poetic forms, her poems nevertheless follow a strictly imposed order, using two- or three-line stanzas with patterned indentations. Her unrhymed lines are lean and brief, connected by enjambment and repetition. The reader senses a rigorous self-imposed discipline underlying the rich images and tropes. The result is delight and instruction. Horace would be pleased.

PUBLISHED WORKS BY MARTHA SERPAS

BOOKS

Côte Blanche (2002)
The Dirty Side of the Storm (2007)
The Diener: Poems (2015)

EDITED VOLUME

Improbable Worlds: An Anthology of Texas and Louisiana Poets (2011)

FILM

Veins in the Gulf (2012)

WORKS CITED

Bloom, Harold. Foreword. *Côte Blanche*. Kalamazoo, Mich.: New Issues Poetry and Prose, 2002.

Louisiana Book Festival. Podcast, 2012.

Serpas, Martha. "A Corollary." *The Dirty Side of the Storm*. New York: Norton, 2007.

———. "Crossing." *The Diener*. Baton Rouge: Louisiana State University Press, 2015.

———. "The Diener." *The Diener*. Baton Rouge: Louisiana State University Press, 2015.

———. "Eulogy." *The Dirty Side of the Storm*. New York: Norton, 2007.

———. "Fais Do-Do." *The Dirty Side of the Storm*. New York: Norton, 2007.

———. "A Future with Hope." *The Dirty Side of the Storm*. New York: Norton, 2007.

———. "Psalm at High Tide." *The Dirty Side of the Storm*. New York: Norton, 2007.

———. "Tinsel." *The Dirty Side of the Storm*. New York: Norton, 2007.

———. "To the Landlady." *The Dirty Side of the Storm*. New York: Norton, 2007.

James Wilcox's Tula Springs

Serious Comedy

Tula Springs, Louisiana, is a small town across the border from Mississippi. The town, its people, and their odd lives, bordering on the bizarre, are the creation of James Wilcox, who has set six novels there. In two other novels, Tula Springs's residents visit New York. The fictional world Wilcox has created, and that he treats with affectionate humor and thoughtful scrutiny, has won the warm regard of his many readers.

The heart of Tula Springs is the Sonny Boy Bargain Store, although for real shopping most people go to the mall across the state border. Next to the bargain store is "a tin-roofed Laundromat, then three empty buildings, one of which—the old wooden hotel built by the lumber company—had a sign promising that it would soon be the home of Jojo's Health Food Emporium (the sign had been promising that for the past two years)" (*Modern Baptists* pt. 1, chap. 1). Tula Springs is "Baptist, puritanical, its houses either dowdy or plain" (pt. 2, chap. 17). It has no police force.

The population of Tula Springs is small but colorful, beginning with people's names and extending through their personalities and relationships. There is Burma LaSteele, who works for a time at Sonny Boy with Toinette, whose name is short for Antoinette, although her tastes bear little resemblance to those of the queen of France. Then there are Miss Undine, Mayor Binwanger, Mrs. Danbar (pronounced "Demmer," although nobody knows why), and F.X. (which stands for Francis Xavier, the name given to him by his mother, an Italian woman who liked saints). Even places have surprising names. In addition to the Sonny Boy store, there are Flat Avenue, Slocum's Tub-A-Rama, Ulmer Foods, and Bulgar Barbeque Service Two. And it is worth noting that there are no springs in Tula Springs.

Readers often have a hard time fitting Wilcox's treatment of his eccentric characters into a neatly defined category. Some say he is writing comedy of manners, that gently mocking genre that finds humor in the conventions and behavior of society. Others say his work is closer to satire, which, through sarcasm and irony, paints society with less restraint and broader strokes. Those who recognize his settings and his characters simply label him "a southern writer." A case can be made for all three descriptions, as there is no denying that his narratives are witty, clever, downright funny. And the courteous, gracious manner that he exhibits in person, which is clearly reflected in his fiction, is quintessentially southern.

Despite some readers' ambivalence about how he and his work should be classified, there is widespread agreement about his significance as a writer. At Louisiana State University, he served as Robert Penn Warren Professor from 2004 to 2007, then as Donald and Velvia Crumbley Professor for the next three years. In 2008 the university recognized him as the Distinguished Research Master of Arts, Humanities, and Social Sciences. He won an LSU Distinguished Faculty Award in 2009 and the next year was given the MacCurdy Distinguished Professorship. He was the recipient of an ATLAS grant for 2007–8. Outside of academia, Wilcox has been honored by the Louisiana Center for the Book with its prestigious Louisiana Writer Award, and in 1986 he was a recipient of a Guggenheim fellowship. Writers such as Toni Morrison, Walker Percy, and Anne Tyler have sung his praises. Harold Bloom even included his *Modern Baptists* in his Western canon.

The distinctive character of Wilcox's fiction comes from his comedic perception of his surroundings that ultimately is rendered in absurd, bizarre, and always humorous depictions of people's traditions, assumptions, and social hierarchies. He is not writing sociology or history or biography, but his imaginary places and people reflect those he has known. Growing up in Hammond, Louisiana, Wilcox had ample opportunity to observe the manners and mores of small-town South Louisiana, and much of his work is based on what he saw and heard there. He says that he usually has to make adjustments to his observations, but some characters and events "are right out of the newspaper" (telephone interview).

Much of the wit and humor in Wilcox's fiction are the result of surprise. Sentences, for example, often fail to fulfill the reader's anticipation. Instead, they do the unexpected by providing information that is incongruous with what has gone before. In *Miss Undine's Living Room*, we are told that Emile Deshotel "was a radiologist who was an authority on stamps and General Custer" (chap. 4). In *Heavenly Days*, Lou, who writes a monthly column for the North American Bassoon Society, "ekes out the necessary [number of] words by grafting a few facts about how pink hydrangeas can be turned blue (sprinkle aluminum onto the soil) onto an item about a Waco bassoonist who tends a hummingbird garden" (chap. 1). Sometimes the details are not merely surprising; they can also seem irrelevant. Mrs. Coco, in *North Gladiola*, "immersed herself in culture, studying French with a retired lady professor who, during a field trip to the opera in New Orleans, ate an innocent-looking oyster that led, via several complications, to her demise" (chap. 1). Sometimes statements are simply bizarre, like the explanation in *Modern Baptists* that "the reason Mr. Pickens let him live there—it wasn't that big a house, just one bedroom with a den, which was where F.X. slept—was because Mr. Pickens had a mole on his back that looked sort of like a fat New Jersey" (chap. 1). The reader has no way to predict where any given sentence is headed. The result: surprise and delight.

Misunderstandings among characters are another source of amusement. In *Plain and Normal*, a novel in which nobody is plain or normal, when Carlos says he is a scholar studying the Adams family, Edwina thinks he means the family in the television comedy. And in

Polite Sex, Emily's parents refuse to be disabused of the notion that her husband is a rich man since his name is Vanderbilt. As Wilcox points out: "Language is ambiguous, and we make assumptions that may be wrong. Rarely do we say precisely what we mean" (telephone interview).

A particularly significant though subtle motif in the novels is change. Tula Springs over time alters demographically, economically, and physically. The population becomes more diverse, the economy stronger, and long-standing family businesses are replaced by chain stores. Even Sonny Boy Bargain Store is bought out and its popular candy counter closed.

The changes, however, do not bring greater peace and happiness. Instead, people continue to feel disappointed and disoriented. As the quotation from Hebrews that serves as the epigraph to *North Gladiola* points out, "These all died in faith, not having received what was promised . . . having acknowledged that they were strangers and exiles on the earth." Even their own homes sometimes fail to offer the stability they desire. In that novel, for example, the Coco home has been sawed in half to make room for a new building. Gretchen Dambar, in *Sort of Rich*, moves to a new home in Louisiana, hoping to be free of the distractions of New York but without success, and Lou Jones, in *Heavenly Days*, feels as if her own expensive home is some sort of public space. As Scott Romine points out in *The Real South*, Wilcox's characters move about (usually in cars) "to find a place where they belong" (chap. 5). They search in different ways for some meaningful action that will lead to a center, a still core that offers stability and confirms their identity. Indeed, it is not too much to say that they search for a spiritual home that continually eludes them.

Their searches take a variety of forms. Donna Lee Keely urges her mother (and others) to get her head "out of the sand" and learn something about real life. She tries to broaden Burma LaSteele's horizons by giving her high-toned books to read and introducing her to the world of nature. Burma, in turn, tries to assist the needy, or those who in her judgment are needy, by giving away money from her late husband's lottery winnings. The three dominant means of finding redemption, however, are music, several different varieties of religion, and academic study. While all three offer meaningful experiences, in inept hands they can become twisted, even ludicrous. While Wilcox ideally holds each to be of value, when he depicts their distortions they become comical. Serious but comical.

Several Tula Springs characters try to bring order and meaning to their bewildering lives through music, an art form that has long held an important place in Wilcox's life. Although he wrote stories when he was young, even completing an introduction to a novel (that never got written), throughout most of his childhood he was headed in another professional direction. As a member of a musical family (his father held a PhD in music and served as head of the music department at Southeastern Louisiana University), Wilcox played piano, organ, and cello from an early age, and by the time he was in high school he was playing cello with the Baton Rouge Symphony Orchestra. He might have extended that experience into a professional career, but after entering and winning local and regional string competitions, he went to St. Louis to compete at the national level and recognized that he did not have the deep commitment that it takes to play professionally. Instead, he moved on to Yale University, where he studied under famed poet and fiction writer Robert Penn Warren. Today he keeps his music alive by playing four-hand piano pieces by the great composers with friends at musical evenings that he enjoys at his home.

Typical of his characters whose lives revolve around music is Lou Jones, in *Heavenly Days*, who is described by her husband as a cheerleader who could "whip out a bassoon and play Hindemith—from memory" (26). Her dissertation was a study of Schoenberg's use of the Lydian mode, an arcane topic even among musicians. She writes a monthly column for the North American Bassoon Society newsletter called "Notes from Up and Down the Staff" and makes a trip to her hometown to deliver an address on the family of wind instruments. In this one novel there are references to Mahler's *Resurrection Symphony*, to Dame Myra Hess playing the *Hammerklavier*, and to a host of composers, including Beethoven, Bruckner, Mozart, Schubert, and Wagner.

Mrs. Coco, in *North Gladiola,* is another who turns to music for solace and meaning. She plays an eighteenth-century cello that she had bought "in 1959 from a failed waiter in New Orleans, who subsequently blossomed out happily as a Mary Kay Cosmetics representative" (chap. 1). She works ceaselessly to bring high culture to Tula Springs and, as part of her efforts, manages a string quartet that performs where it can, including the grand opening of the new BurgerMat and Dick's China Nights, a Chinese restaurant seeking to increase patronage, where "they found themselves in competition with gunshots and tire squeals through the gold-flecked fiberboard that separated the restaurant from the Leon Cinema" (chap. 7).

The protagonist of *Guest of a Sinner,* Eric, is a professional pianist who both teaches and performs. He has been reviewed positively in the *Village Voice* for his skills as an accompanyist. Through him Wilcox even analyzes various selections. As Eric comments: "Rosa wants the Prokofiev slowed down to a crawl. It's ludicrous. She has no idea what that sonata's all about. It's a youthful, joyous, almost barbaric free-for-all" (chap. 16). When he attends a performance by Ida Grossman, we are told: "Her recent recital at Merkin Hall had left Eric weak with admiration. As far as he was concerned, no one played Scriabin better—and her Schumann, the *Kreisleriana,* was the most intense emotional experience he had had in years" (chap. 7).

Sometimes characters are not themselves musicians but sense that music has the capacity to restore their spirits. Mr. Pickens, in *Modern Baptists,* dutifully attends an opera. "Though bored out of his mind, he was mature enough to realize that great music such as this was supposed to have a good effect on you, whether you liked it or not; so he endured it." Later the reader learns, "He would have liked to see the last act of the opera—not because he was enjoying the singing but because he thought if you were going to absorb culture, it didn't count unless you absorbed the whole thing" (chap. 7).

Various types of religious belief offer highly attractive but not always effective ways of coping. Wilcox's own religious background was varied, as his mother was Roman Catholic and his father attended the Methodist church, where he conducted the choir. On Sundays, Wilcox attended Mass, then played the organ for the Methodists, associating him with both denominations, and in his fiction both Catholics and Protestants get their fair share of commentary.

Mr. Pickens, who goes down a number of paths in search of his purpose and calling, is one of the latter. He decides to become a preacher and open a church for modern Baptists. His reformed institution "would be guided by reason and logic. Everyone could drink in moderation. Everyone could dance and pet as long as they were fifteen—well, maybe sixteen or seventeen. At thirty, if you still weren't married, you could sleep with someone, and it wouldn't be a sin—that is, as long as you loved that person. If you hit forty and were still single, you'd be eligible for adultery not being a sin, as long as no children's feelings got hurt and it was kept very discreet" (*Modern Baptists* chap. 20).

In the same novel Mr. Keely hosts his men's Bible class and invites his daughter, Donna Lee, to attend as a guest. When Dr. McFlug reads aloud a passage from Nehemiah describing a feast, she challenges him first about the ethics of the speaker, who, she claims, kept the best food for himself and left others with only bread, and then about the size of the ox that had been slaughtered for the feast. In response Dr. McFlug proclaims, "If God willed . . . an ox could weigh three hundred pounds." And when another member of the group suggests that in the context of the reading *bread* probably means something else, Dr. McFlug staunchly maintains: "Either you believe what's written there, just like it says, or you don't. Either it's the word of God or it isn't" (*Modern Baptists* chap. 16). Old-time religion, not a reformed one, is Dr. McFlug's answer to life's quandaries.

A third belief system is found in *Heavenly Days*, in which Waist Watch, a weight loss center, has the Ten Commandments posted on the restroom door. Its employees get discounts for Scripture spinning, which involves virtually biking through the Holy Land, and

Couples in Christ, one of its new programs that involves "exorcising your mutual hatred with kick-boxing."

While fundamentalism and new age belief systems may be spoofed in Wilcox's fiction, respect for thoughtful religious belief deepens what at first glance may seem to be the depiction of simplistic theology. Wilcox's own biblical knowledge is extensive, as is evident in the frequent quotations throughout his work. Another serious note comes early in the novels, as most begin with an epigraph from literature or Scripture, signaling that what follows is no simple comedy. Even *Modern Baptists,* which obviously has its share of wit and caricature, opens with a quotation from Psalm 89: "Remember how short my time is." *Miss Undine's Living Room* begins with both a quotation from the *Information Please Almanac* and the well-known line from the Book of Ruth "and where thou lodgest, I will lodge." Comments by C. S. Lewis introduce *Guest of a Sinner, Heavenly Days,* and *Hunk City.* Even William James gets quoted in *Polite Sex.*

Some characters turn to academia and scholarly study for answers to life's dilemmas. They explore a world that Wilcox knows well. Although he had hoped to begin publishing his own fiction after graduation from Yale, he instead moved to New York, where he began working as an editor. The many demands on his time—reading manuscripts and getting agents to send him their best ones—left him constantly working but not writing. At the age of twenty-nine, having yet to publish anything of significance, he made the transition from editing to writing and devoted the next several years in New York to getting his novels published. They were ascetic years but also productive ones. When in 1998 Wilcox had the opportunity to be a visiting writer at Mississippi State University, he added teaching to his professional credentials. Finding that he enjoyed the sustained time on campus, in 2001 he moved to Louisiana State University, where, until recently, he served as head of the creative writing program. Currently he is enjoying a balance of writing and teaching. He describes the latter as being somewhat like being an editor. That is, teaching writing, he says, involves reassuring students that he understands what they are trying to say but at the same time pointing out the gap between what they say and what they mean.

When Wilcox's characters attempt to cultivate the life of the mind, they prove to be no more effective than Mr. Pickens in his efforts to establish a reformed church. In the novels several characters have written or are writing dissertations, a natural target for parody. In addition to Lou Jones's study of Schoenberg's use of the Lydian mode in *Heavenly Days, North Gladiola* features Duk-Soo (duck soup?), a Korean graduate student who also plays in Mrs. Coco's string quartet. He is struggling to complete his dissertation entitled "Heim, Haims, Heimr, Hām: The Semantic Obfuscation of the Tourist's Ultimate Destination." In describing the course of a typical tourist's vacation, he writes:

> Ultimately, if one renders this logic in Hegelian terms . . . the sign "home" is synthesized into a state of apatheia where one is so acclimatized to one's environment that one fails to perceive anything at all. The tourist, having launched out on what we have earlier concluded was a voluntary exile involving a praxis of unfamiliar sights, sounds, and tastes impacting upon him, is now ready to complete the circular paradigm by returning home. Needless to say, the "ideal" home is one in which one is so comfortable that one is not aware of oneself at all, i.e., one is totally un-self-conscious: The self has dissolved. What is this "home" we are talking about, then? Is it not, when we factor in the above, quite simply *der Tod*? (*North Gladiola* chap. 15)

The simple is made complex. That which was clear becomes obfuscated. Thus speaks academia, according to Wilcox.

In *Polite Sex*, Hugh, too, is writing a dissertation. Although he is not especially religious, (he views religion to be full of self-righteousness and sexist bureaucracies), he is studying for a theology degree. One of his papers, an examination of the philosophical hermeneutics of Schleiermacher, received the comment from his professor that Hugh had "an astonishing critical facility whose iconoclasm was balanced by a judicious use of primary source material" (*Polite Sex* 98). Again, academic-speak.

Despite the parodies and gentle satire about academia, the reader cannot help but be impressed by Wilcox's own breadth of learning in general and vocabulary in particular. Allusions to a wide range of scholarship abound. In *North Gladiola* alone, there are references to Barth, Tillich and Bonhoeffer, Irenaeus, Augustine and Ruether, Gutiérrez and Schillebeeckx, all theologians of a scholarly bent. *Polite Sex* refers to Seneca's *Medea* and *Hercules Furens*, Corneille's *La Mort de Pompée*, and Racine's *Phèdre*, Boethius, Troubadour poetry from the eleventh century, C. S. Lewis's *The Allegory of Love*, Eliot's *Middlemarch*, Woolf's *The Voyage Out*, trecento art, and objective correlatives.

Such scholarly references reflect an impressive intellectual background that is underscored by Wilcox's use of out-of-the-ordinary words. In *Hunk City*, for example, the reader comes across *oleomysonary, consanguine, riparian, plasticine,* and *arsenokoetis. Guest of a Sinner* uses *toque, moonwort, counterpane, asperges, swivet,* and *nacreous. North Gladiola* is particularly rich, with the use of *rhea, foulard, veld, bespoke* (referring to handmade shoes), *ostinato, puce,* and *oleaginous.* Like the scholarly allusions, such unusual language reflects an extraordinarily well-educated and thoughtful writer.

The people who live in James Wilcox's fictive Tula Springs are, in the end, amusing, eccentric, and endearing, but they are also something more. They are drifting individuals yearning for something permanent and real that remains just beyond their grasp. Their efforts to find answers to the riddles of their lives appear laughable to the casual reader, but on second glance they are all too recognizable. In them the thoughtful reader sees something of the human condition, something of the self, a serious comedy.

PUBLISHED WORKS BY JAMES WILCOX

Modern Baptists (1983)
North Gladiola (1985)
Miss Undine's Living Room (1987)
Sort of Rich (1989)
Polite Sex (1991)
Guest of a Sinner (1993)
Plain and Normal (1998)
Heavenly Days (2003)
Hunk City (2007)
Three short stories published in the *New Yorker* (1981–86)

WORKS CITED

Romine, Scott. *The Real South: Southern Narrative in the Age of Cultural Reproduction.* Baton Rouge: Louisiana State University Press, 2008. Kindle edition.

Wilcox, James. *Guest of a Sinner.* 1993. Rpr. Baton Rouge: Louisiana State University Press, 2004. Kindle edition.

———. *Heavenly Days.* New York: Viking Penguin, 2003. Kindle edition.

———. *Miss Undine's Living Room.* 1987. Rpr. Baton Rouge: Louisiana State University Press, 2001. Kindle edition.

———. *Modern Baptists.* 1983. Rpr. Baton Rouge: Louisiana State University Press, 2006. Kindle edition.

———. *North Gladiola.* 1985. Rpr. Baton Rouge: Louisiana State University Press, 2000. Kindle edition.

———. *Polite Sex.* Boston: Little, Brown, 1991.

———. Telephone interview, March 18, 2015.

The Newcomers

When the Louisiana Endowment for the Humanities decided to compile an online encyclopedia of Louisiana writers as part of its KnowLouisiana (KnowLA) project, nobody dreamed that it would run to 222 entries and continue to grow. The fact is that Louisiana has always been rich in writers, its literary history stretching back to George Washington Cable and Kate Chopin, hosting Sherwood Anderson and William Faulkner for a time, then teeming with a throng of mid-twentieth-century and early-twenty-first century poets, novelists, and playwrights. There has never been a shortage of Louisianans with literary gifts, and current trends promise an abundant supply of young and upcoming scribblers, some of them native to the state, some adoptees, some visitors, all of them touched by the unique culture of Louisiana. Some of them work in genres rarely visited by established writers. Ashley Weaver, for example, writes in a distinctly Agatha Christie vein that isn't found in the fictional worlds of her contemporaries. Some, like Wiley Cash, mingle their Louisiana experiences with those of their home states, producing a blended sense of place. All of them bring fresh voices and viewpoints to the scene. Here is an overview of some of those receiving recent positive press and attention.

Wiley Cash

Although not a Louisiana native, Wiley Cash recognizes the influence that the state had on him while pursuing his PhD degree at the University of Louisiana at Lafayette (ULL). Particularly important was the opportunity to study with Ernest Gaines, who, he says, had an immeasurable effect on his writing and on his life in general.

The idea for Cash's first novel, *A Land More Kind than Home,* was an African American literature class he took at ULL. One day the professor brought in a news story about a young African American boy with autism who was smothered during a church healing service in a storefront church on Chicago's South Side. Unable to forget the incident, Cash moved the setting to western North Carolina, his home environment, and it became the story of an entire community. It is a mystery thriller and an emotional tale of a family and a town dealing with evil acts that masquerade as God's will. It was hailed by the *New York Times* as "mesmerizing," the reviewer saying that it reads "as if Cormac McCarthy decided to rewrite Harper Lee's *To Kill a Mockingbird*" (qtd. in *Richmond Times-Dispatch*). It became a *New York Times* best seller, *New York Times* Notable Book of 2012, winner of the Thomas Wolfe Memorial Book Prize, and the Barnes & Noble Discover Great New Writers Selection.

Using multiple narrators, as Ernest Gaines had done in *A Gathering of Old Men, A Land More Kind than Home* reflects the importance that a sense of place holds for Cash. Talking with *Fiction Writers Review,* he explains the impact place has on him: "I loved living in Lafayette, Louisiana, for five years during graduate school. The language, food, and landscape were different from any other place I'd ever visited, and while I lived there I took every opportunity to immerse myself in it. I think it made me a better writer because it made me more curious about North Carolina, the place I call home" (Wetherell 7). In an interview with National Public Radio, he says, "Every time I put pen to paper, it's an act of trying to reclaim a place I love, and a place that I miss and a place that I get to live in whenever I sit down to work" (Martin).

Cash's second novel, *This Dark Road to Mercy,* tells the story of two young sisters kidnapped by their wayward father despite his having signed away his legal rights to their care. Cash explains that it is about "looking back at things that we once believed to be true—whether it's about our families or about ourselves or about our national obsessions—and asking ourselves, 'Am I believing correctly? Am I seeing this with clear eyes?'" (Martin). Like his first novel, the style can be described as Southern Gothic, although some readers felt that it lacked the surprise and emotional intensity of its predecessor. Nevertheless, it became a national best seller, an Amazon Book of the Month, and the *Library Journal* Top Ten Book of 2012 and garnered a long list of other prestigious awards.

Wiley Cash and his wife now live in West Virginia, where he teaches fiction writing and American literature at Bethany College.

Ashley Mace Havird

Ashley Mace Havird grew up on a tobacco farm in South Carolina, a landscape and people that she wanted to write a long piece about. The upshot is her novel *Lightningstruck,* set in Marion County, South Carolina, during the height of the tobacco industry. Taking place in the mid-1960s, it is also the height of the civil rights era. The social upheavals of the day as well as the stresses of growing up and dealing with family, peers, and small-town issues are all narrated by eleven-year-old Etta McDaniels. As she confronts (and questions) racism, the land, and family in this coming-of-age story, her evolving understanding of tolerance, morality, and social justice powerfully reflects the complexities of growing up and coming to understand our world. The novel won the Ferrol Sams Award for Fiction. Lee Morgan, professor emeritus of English at Centenary College, says, "*Lightningstruck* is a finely crafted novel which will make readers hope to see another from this talented writer—soon."

Known as a prize-winning poet before she published her novel, Havird points out the difference between working in the two genres. "As a lyric poet," she says, "I try to capture a moment, a scene, that perhaps contains a story or hints of a story in much the same way that a documentary photograph implies a story. Writing a novel is more like painting a mural, one that extends for several blocks or longer" (Christie). However, many of her poems grow out of the same time and place as *Lightningstruck*. Some others, like those in *The Garden of the Fugitives,* which won the X. J. Kennedy Prize, reflect her travels, moving as far afield as Pompeii and the Cayman Islands. Regardless of the setting, her poetry, like her novel, addresses tensions in human relationships, with the environment, and even with animals. Havird's two other books of poetry are *Sleeping with Animals* and *Dirt Eaters,* the second of which won the 2008 South Carolina Poetry Initiative Prize.

She is working on a new novel set in the future rather than the past. She is also interested in writing another book of poems, this one about animals. She now lives in Shreveport, Louisiana, with her husband.

Anne L. Simon

Another newcomer on the scene is Anne Simon, a retired judge from the Sixteenth Judicial District. Drawing on her courtroom experiences in Iberia, St. Martin, and St. Mary Parishes, some of them bizarre and exotic and most all of them complicated, she has fashioned three mystery novels set in that area. The narratives of *Blood in the Lake, Blood in the Cane Field,* and *Blood of the Believers* are complexly plotted, with character development that shows the author's long experience with the exotic mix of Cajun, African American, Native American, and Anglo cultures that interact to form unusual alliances and conflicts. A longtime bird-watcher, Simon draws on her familiarity with the natural world of South Louisiana, creating detailed descriptions of its rivers, swamps, flora and fauna, and of course, its birds.

The mystery of *Blood in the Lake* is precipitated by the discovery of the body of the patriarch of the Boudreaux family at the bottom of Lake Peigneur. His granddaughter, a law student, becomes embroiled in the search for the murderer, a search that results in dangerous consequences for her and her little brother. It also leads to a love affair with her boss and mentor. In *Blood in the Cane Field,* public defender John Clark III is called on to defend a barely eighteen-year-old visibly black man who claims he is white. In the process he meets a Mississippi girl with a past who makes him question his resolution to avoid commitment. As the mystery unfolds, the two of them are brought into conflict with political influence and criminal power.

Asked why she turned to writing novels in her retirement, she replied: "For 30 years on the bench I have watched ordinary people in extraordinary circumstances. The novel gives me license to tell their stories, explore their issues, and imagine what has taken place outside the courtroom in our fascinating corner of the world" (personal interview).

Although Anne Simon has not been reviewed by national publications, she has developed a loyal local following of readers who enjoy her South Louisiana mysteries. She lives in New Iberia, Louisiana.

Katy Simpson Smith

Katy Simpson Smith garnered notice from prestigious reviewers with her debut novel, *The Story of Land and Sea.* Her second, *Free Men,* was equally well received. Both are set in postcolonial America, their attention to the authenticity of details reflecting Smith's doctorate in history; the writing testifies to her MFA degree earned from the Bennington Writing Seminars in Vermont. Both novels were preceded in publication by her nonfiction study, *We Have Raised All of You: Motherhood in the South, 1750–1835,* derived from her doctoral dissertation.

Asked about her dual interests in history and fiction, Smith says: "Historical fiction was a chance for me to explore things I knew nothing about. What's it like to be a grandfather, for example? And what if that sympathetic grandfather also was a slaveholder? Fiction lets me explore the fluid boundaries between good and evil that exist in all of us" (qtd. in Waddington). Lest her use of the term *historical fiction* suggest that her work is less than serious, it should be noted that Carmela Ciuraru, a reviewer for the *New York Times,* points out that

Smith "immerses the reader beyond period verisimilitude and sensory detail, taking her [the reader] deep into the collective psyche of another era." The *Huffington Post* says that her historical vision "flawlessly blends the beauty and idealism of American independence with the hypocrisy and devastation."

Why has she set both novels in the postcolonial period? In an interview with *Parnassus Musing,* Smith comments that it invites examination because it was "the awkward adolescent stage of our country. So much of the ideology that seems entrenched now was just getting tossed around in those years as people in positions of power made choices that would affect women, the enslaved, and Native groups for centuries. But in the 1780s and 1790s you can still glimpse a fluidity to human relationships. There are still forks in this nation's road, and it's exciting as a historian and a writer to witness all those possibilities" ("Katy Simpson Smith"). It is no surprise, then, that her novels explore questions of identity, guilt, morality, and coming of age.

Smith has received praise that seldom comes to writers so young, but she has also been criticized for sometimes adopting narrative structures that allow the reader to know what is going to happen long before it does. And although readers often comment on her "memorable images," some see them as overextended, making her style sometimes impenetrable.

Ashley Weaver

As the branch manager of the Allen Parish Libraries, Ashley Weaver would seem to be an unlikely writer of mystery novels that inevitably make the reader think of Agatha Christie. So far she has produced three in three years, *Murder at the Brightwell, Death Wears a Mask,* and *A Most Novel Revenge.* All three have as their heroine the plucky would-be detective Amory Ames.

Murder at the Brightwell was nominated in 2015 for the Edgar Award for Best First Novel. It is set in 1932 at a British seaside resort where a group of well-to-do (and entertaining) aristocrats are on holiday. When one of them is murdered, Amory turns sleuth looking for the villain. Multiple red herrings throw the reader off course, and additional wrongdoings heighten the suspense. The one mystery Amory is unable to solve is her own conflicted feelings toward her husband and her former fiancé, both of whom turn up at the Brightwell.

Death Wears a Mask moves to London but picks up where the preceding novel left off. This time Amory is caught up in solving the murder of a guest at a lavish masked ball. And as before, rumors swirl about Milo, Amory's playboy husband. *A Most Novel Revenge* takes place the following year at an English country house to which a group of distinguished guests have been invited by a socialite who threatens to publish a book revealing the secrets of the company, all of whom were present when a murder took place at the same country house some years earlier. Needless to say, a second murder occurs, and Amory sets out to solve it.

It is a glittering society that Weaver describes in her novels. The dialogue of the characters is witty and sharp, and their wardrobes are stylish and elegant. These entertaining, traditional mystery novels make the reader look forward to reading more tales based on the world of Amory Ames.

Ashley Weaver now lives in Oberlin, Louisiana.

Steve Weddle

A voice from North Louisiana comes from Steve Weddle, who grew up on the state line with Arkansas. His novel *Country Hardball*, set in that area, tells stories of people caught in a small rural town that is in a downward spiral economically, socially, and ethically. There are no good options for their lives, though they struggle to surmount their bad luck and past histories. The novel has been called gritty, grim, funny, poignant, tough, and elegant. The *New York Times* hailed Weddle's writing as "downright dazzling" (Stasio).

Although *Country Hardball* is a novel, it is actually eighteen interrelated stories. The characters appear and reappear from story to story, creating a mosaic that is a picture of the town and its culture. In structure and effect,the novel is frequently compared to Sherwood Anderson's *Winesburg, Ohio.* Central to the several narratives is Roy Alison, recently released from jail but still carrying guilt from his teenage years for having caused an accident that resulted in his parents' death. He is returning home determined to do better. What he finds, however, is a depressed, hardscrabble community struggling to cope with life and perhaps improve it. Despite good intentions, he, along with his fellow townsfolk, continues to make bad choices even as he searches for a better life. Weddle tells the stories of the town, dark though they are, with compassion, honesty, and respect.

Weddle claims that he started writing fiction because he was a "terrible student." However, his record suggests otherwise. He received his undergraduate degree from Centenary College of Louisiana, a master of arts from Pittsburgh State University, and his master of fine arts in poetry from Louisiana State University. After LSU, he worked as a journalist and taught. In an interview with *My Bookish Ways,* he admitted that he has always been a writer. It is no surprise, then, that having been influenced by Hemingway and Raymond Carver, he turned to writing fiction, producing numerous short stories, including "South of Bradley," a follow-up story to *Country Hardball.*

Although the novel has received praise from many quarters, some readers have found it difficult to keep so many stories and family trees straight. The author points out, however, that the narrative would not work as a traditional novel. Since it has as much to do with the region as with the people, everything is connected although everything is fragmented.

Asked about how he likes to spend his free time, he admits that when he is not writing he is thinking about writing. His preoccupation takes several forms. He is an active participant in online projects, for one. He is the cofounder (with Jay Stringer) of the crime fiction collective Do Some Damage, the cocreator of the noir magazine

Needle, and a regular instructor at LitReactor.com. He continues to set his fiction in North Louisiana.

Weddle now lives with his family in Virginia.

Ken Wheaton

Ken Wheaton did not set out to be a novelist or a writer of any kind. On the way to finding his calling, he tried to join the air force as a pilot, then explored becoming a marine biologist, finally changing his college major to English. The writing started with his reviews of the cafeteria food at Long Island University–Southampton that featured sharply critical comments about the kitchen staff's attempts to produce Cajun dishes. (He "published" them by posting them on the cafeteria's suggestion board.) A native of Grand Prairie, Louisiana, and born into a large Cajun family, Wheaton knew what was lacking and inauthentic. From food commentaries he moved on to working on the college newspaper, first as a political columnist and later as its editor. The political commentary led him to writing the humorous essay, a genre that at the time he did not connect with fiction. After graduation he worked briefly at newspapers on Long Island before returning home to attend graduate school at the University of Southwestern Louisiana (now the University of Louisiana at Lafayette), where he earned a master's degree in creative writing. Then it was back to New York, where he began work at a trade magazine called *Marine Log*, then worked as a copy editor at TheStreet.com, followed by the same position at *Advertising Age*, later working his way up to managing editor.

The humor he cultivated in his college journalism later found an outlet in his novels. Wheaton claims that when he was younger, he considered fiction to be a serious affair, and it was only at the urging of friends that he began to make the tone of his stories lighter and funnier. In fact, his first novel, *The First Annual Grand Prairie Rabbit Festival*, began, according to Wheaton, in a considerably more serious vein and had to be rewritten with the intention of adding humor.

The result is the story of a priest in a small town in South Louisiana who ministers to a colorful (read outrageous) congregation. When a competing Pentecostal church threatens to steal some of his parishioners, he stages the town's first annual rabbit festival, featuring a crazy cookout, an elephant named Gertie, all the alcohol one can consume, and more. Readers were charmed with the vibrancy, authenticity, and sheer wackiness of the characters and their antics. Some of the initial serious elements remain, however, with the work's consideration of racism, sexual preference, and Christian relationships. The novel even includes some recipes with accompanying explanations.

Wheaton's second novel, *Bacon and Egg Man*, a political satire, was intentionally funny from the outset. Set in the future, it tells the story of a bacon and egg dealer who lives in a culture obsessed with nutrition and health. It is a world that on the surface is tightly controlled but underneath seethes with human corruption and decadence. Because of its subject and its setting, it sometimes seems more forbidding and depressing than funny.

Sweet as Cane, Salty as Tears, Wheaton's third novel, was, he says, an effort "to strike a balance between funny and serious and warm and nostalgic" (Fulco). Like the author himself, the central character, Katherine "Katie-Lee" Fontenot, has been living in New York for decades when she is forced by a freak accident to return to Louisiana and acknowledge the family and roots she has been running from for years. It is a large, sprawling, messy family, leaving the protagonist with conflicting emotions about how she wants to feel about it. The authenticity of the picture Wheaton paints of Cajun culture in the novel has been particularly admired.

Wheaton claims that much of what he writes is taken from life. That leaves an author vulnerable to negative family reactions, but he says that has not been the case for him. But it's not just family that enjoys his novels. He is building a wide audience of approving readers.

WORKS CITED

Centorcelli, Kristin. "Interview: Steve Weddle, Author of *Country Hardball*." *My Bookish Ways* blog, November 20, 2013, www.mybookishways.com/2013/11/interview-steve-weddle-author-of-country-hardball.html.

Childers, Doug. "Fiction Review: *A Land More Kind than Home*." *Richmond Times-Dispatch*, April 15, 2012, *www.richmond.com/entertainment/article_156b8cc5-7c39-5d66-8f79-97a70b0aa6c2.html*.

Christie, Judy. "Ashley Mace Havird Interview." *Shreveport Times*, August 17, 2016.

Ciuraru, Carmela. "Katie Simpson-Smith." *New York Times*, August 27, 2014.

Fallon, Claire. "The Book We're Talking About: 'The Story of Land and Sea' by Katy Simpson Smith." *Huffington Post*, August 20, 2014, www.huffingtonpost.com/2014/08/20/story-of-land-and-sea-kat_n_5694757.html.

Fulco, Richard. "The Dead Thing on the Porch Is the Tooth Fairy: An Interview with Ken Wheaton." *Fiction Writers Review*, December 8, 2014, *http://fictionwritersreview.com/interview/the-dead-thing-on-the-porch-is-the-tooth-fairy-an-interview-with-ken-wheaton/*.

"Katy Simpson Smith Writes Historical Fiction That's Anything but Boring." *Parnassus Musing*, February 18, 2016, https://parnassusmusing.net/2016/02/18/katy-simpson-smith-free-men.

Martin, Rachel. "Gothic Thriller Takes Two Young Girls down a 'Dark Road to Mercy.'" National Public Radio interview, February 2, 2014, *www.npr.org/2014/02/02/265706063/gothic-thriller*-takes-two-young-girls-down-a-dark-road-to-mercy.

Morgan, Lee. Personal interview, August 3, 2016.

Simon, Anne. Personal interview, November 11, 2015.

Stasio, Marilyn. "Without a Trace: Sara Paretsky's 'Critical Mass,' and More." Review of Steve Weddle's *Country Hardball*. *New York Times*, November 15, 2013, Sunday Book Review, www.nytimes.com/2013/11/17/books/review/sara-paretskys-critical-mass-and-more.html.

Waddington, Chris. "Katie Simpson-Smith Grabs National Attention for Grand Debut Novel—and Pop Star Payday." *New Orleans Times-Picayune*, August 29, 2014, *http://nola.com/books/ndex.ssf/2014/08/katy-simpson-smith-grabs-natio.html*.

Wetherell, Brad. "Many Souths: An Interview with Wiley Cash." *Fiction Writers Review*, April 17, 2012, *www.fictionwritersreview.com/interview/many-souths-an-interview-with-wiley-cash*.

Index